Money Skills for Teens

10 Essential Skills Every Teenager Must Know
About Personal Finance and Money Management
- Your Guide to Making, Saving, Budgeting and
Investing Money

Lindsey Sterling

Table of Contents

A Special Note to Parents

T hank you for choosing to invest in your teenager's financial education by picking up this book. It's a decision that can have a profound impact on their future.

We understand the importance of your role in supporting your teen's learning journey. As they dive into these pages, we encourage you to be there for them, ready to answer questions, offer guidance, and share your own valuable experiences. Your involvement makes all the difference.

Remember, this book isn't just for your teenager; it's a valuable resource for you as well. It can help in navigating essential conversations about money with your teen. Use it as a reference to initiate discussions about budgeting, saving, investing, and financial responsibility. The insights within these pages can make these conversations more engaging and productive and strengthen the bond between you and your teen.

Don't forget to download the bonus workbook that accompanies this book, found in the Introduction section on Page 5. It's designed to complement the reading experience and provide practical exercises to reinforce the concepts that are taught throughout the book. Together, you and your teen can explore the world of money management, setting them on a path toward financial success.

We want to acknowledge how amazing you are for actively seeking ways to improve your teenager's financial literacy. Your commitment as a parent is truly commendable.

Thank you for being an essential part of your teen's journey to financial empowerment. We're excited to have you on board and confident that, together, we can equip your teenager with the money skills they need to thrive.

Introduction

Who Am I and Why I Wrote This Book

Let me start by expressing my appreciation and gratitude for choosing to invest your time and trust in my book. I wanted to kick things off by sharing a bit about myself and my motivations for writing this book.

As a self-taught mentor and passionate educator, my journey has been driven by curiosity and a deep commitment to empowering others. Facing a lack of educational resources and guidance in my youth, my story is not one of conventional academic pathways. I'm not a self-proclaimed money "guru" with a string of degrees or accolades. Instead I excelled through self-study and perseverance, influenced by my own personal experiences and struggles. I know firsthand how daunting it can be to navigate the world of money without a roadmap. That's exactly what compelled me to write this book – to be the guide I wished I had as a teenager.

I've continued to grow my knowledge and experience through volunteering. As I engaged with local teens and grew my connections with the community, I realized how few resources are available for young people when it comes to learning about money. I saw bright, capable young minds eager to learn but lacking the tools to do so. It further ignited my mission to bridge the gap between knowledge and its seekers, particularly among the youth. I strongly believe that education is not just about formal degrees but about the continuous pursuit of knowledge and the ability to share it with others. I'm passionate about understanding and teaching people. And feel an immense sense of achievement in seeing someone's eyes light up when they grasp a new concept.

But my motivation goes beyond just giving back to the community. It's also deeply personal. My role as a parent amplifies my dedication to fostering knowledge. I'm driven by the desire to nurture a brighter future where the next generation are better equipped to make informed, confident decisions. This book is part of my legacy – not just for my son but for every teenager who feels lost in the world of money and finances.

Writing this book was a way of taking all those years of self-taught lessons and experiences and turning them into something valuable for others. Financial literacy is a crucial skill for everyone, regardless of their background. It's about more than just money; it's about making informed decisions, planning for the future, and gaining the confidence to take control of your life.

So whether you're a teen just starting to think about money, a parent looking to guide your child, or anyone in between, this book can be a helpful asset. It's a compilation of many essential concepts and resources and taught in a way that's easy to understand and apply. The hope is that by sharing this knowledge and experience, this book can help you avoid the pitfalls that I, and many others, have already encountered. And set you on a path to financial success.

Who Should Read This Book

First off, *congratulations* for picking up this book! It's a smart and brave step in setting yourself up for success. "Money Skills for Teens" is a book that's been written and tailored for teens just like you. If you want to learn more about money but find the whole topic a bit overwhelming, this book is for you. It's for those who may be at a pivotal point in their life, ready to start mastering their money skills but unsure where to begin. Or those who feel like they're standing at the threshold of independence but being held back by a lack of basic financial skills.

You're not alone. It's a proven fact that schools often skip out on teaching these crucial money lessons, leaving you unprepared for the real-world financial responsibilities that await. Maybe you've seen friends or family handle their cash like pros and wondered, "How do they do that?" This book was designed to help empower you, not just as an observer but as someone who can also be confident and in control of their money.

Do terms like "budgeting," "credit scores," and "investing" sound like a foreign language to you? Have you downloaded a money app and ended up even more confused? Maybe you've thought, "I'm just not good with money." Well, this book is here to change that. It's about proving to you that making, managing, and saving money isn't just for teens who are math whizzes or in all those AP classes. It's for anyone willing to put in the work and effort to build a better future for themselves.

Now, let's be real; if you're not willing to put in the effort or challenge yourself to learn new things, or if you don't think it's worth your time, then this book probably isn't for you. If you have no interest in this book's topics or content, you likely won't gain much from it. Or if you simply aren't focusing on your future yet and how developing your money skills can improve it, that's ok too! This book will always be here, whenever you're ready.

But, for those who feel like they're missing out on essential money skills, this book is your stepping stone from confusion to confidence. Whether it's figuring out how to make money, saving up for something big, getting better at managing your money, or just understanding how money works, we've got you covered.

You're obviously interested in learning more about money; that's why you picked up this book, right? But maybe you're cautious or hesitant to dive into a new subject. After all, you've probably got a lot on your plate already with high school! We understand. You don't want to waste time on stuff that won't actually help. That's why this book offers practical, real-world advice that's easy to follow and written with a teenager in mind. No fluff, just real talk and hands-on exercises you can use right away to get better with money.

So, if you're ready to turn your doubts into action, your questions into answers, and your wishful thinking into real plans, you're in the perfect place. Let's help get you from "wait, what?", to "yeah, I got this" and lay down a path to dominate your money skills and level up your independence. Are you in?!

Download Your Bonus Workbook

As a special thank you, I've included a bonus digital workbook that was designed to enrich your reading experience. It's a practical tool that goes hand in hand with this book. It's meant to enhance your journey and keep you engaged as you learn more about money. Inside, you'll find over 25 pages of helpful resources, such as:

Hands-On Exercises: Engage with interactive activities that bring the book's lessons to life.
Cheat Sheets: Quick-reference guides to help you recall key concepts and tips & tricks effortlessly.
Useful Templates: Ready-to-use templates to simplify your financial planning and decision-making.

… And more! Side hustle ideas, resume templates, helpful checklists and a monthly budget planner. You won't want to miss out on these bonus resources. For your convenience, the workbook will come in a full-color PDF *fillable* format. You may also print it if you prefer. Please note, that the PDF is best used on a computer or laptop. To access and download the workbook, simply scan the QR code below or follow the provided link.

Or Access The Link At:
https://bit.ly/msft-bonus

1

Money Talks - Why You Should Listen

You've probably heard the term "money talks?" But have you ever thought about what that actually means? In this chapter, we'll start with some basics and hopefully get you thinking about why it's important to (hypothetically) listen to what money is trying to tell you. We'll also give you a sneak peek into what you have to look forward to in this book and why you won't want to miss out on the knowledge bombs that each chapter has to offer.

Did you know a survey found that 93% of teens believe that financial knowledge and skills are needed to achieve their life goals?[1] 93%! You should pat yourself on the back for being one of the 93% who is actually taking action and finding resources to improve your financial knowledge.

Did you also know that another survey found that 3 out of 4 Gen Z teens don't feel confident or knowledgeable about personal finances?[2] That's 75%!

Here's another scary fact: 41% of students said they did not have any classes in high school that taught financial skills.[3] It's no wonder you probably feel completely out of the loop or totally lost at the thought of money and finances. You're not alone. But that's why you're here, right? We're going to knock down those barriers and get you up-to-speed on all things money! You should feel excited at the thought of becoming *that* friend, who everyone comes to for money advice, or *that* teen that everyone is secretly jealous of. You will get there, and this book will help.

Let's Spill the Tea

Imagine a world where cash flowed like your favorite influencer's endless story updates. Where every 'like' could be a dollar in your pocket, and every share could be a step closer to your financial dreams. Sounds intriguing, right? Well, guess what? Nowadays, understanding money isn't just about counting cash; it's about catching up with the financial buzz, breaking down myths, and getting the real 'tea' on how money works. So, let's spill it, sip it, and set you on the path to becoming the money mastermind we know you can be.

In its most basic form, money is a medium of exchange or a way to trade things and services. But today, it's so much more than just coins and bills. It's a digital entity, a credit score, and an intricate part of our daily lives. Money has gone through a significant transformation since its early days until today.

Today, money goes beyond its traditional use as a means of exchange. Money now serves as a store of wealth. Money is everywhere. So, you must understand what it is, what it's for, and why you need it.

How Money Has Evolved

Money, as we know it, has come a long way from its roots. In the past, people used systems to trade and exchange goods for other goods. However, this often posed a challenge due to the concept of "double coincidence." One individual has to have exactly what the other individual wants in order for a trade to work. Otherwise, neither individual will get what they need. As you can imagine, this made the "barter" system pretty limited. Because of this, humans realized that a standardized medium of exchange was necessary. This situation led to the creation of coins and, eventually, dollar bills.

Fast forward to today, and we're now dealing with a variety of digital payment methods and cryptocurrencies like Bitcoin. Money is now universally accepted, as you know. Ultimately, it simplifies the purchasing process and makes it easy and convenient for us to exchange, really anything! Money still works in the same way. The difference is instead of using salt, bird feathers, or cattle, we can now store our money in our pockets or phones. Imagine what our ancestors would think if they could see us today!

The Time Value of Money

Have you ever stopped to think about the value of money? Or how it could change over time? You're probably sitting there thinking, "uhm, no." I'm going to challenge you to dive into an interesting concept with me. The idea is, that a dollar today is worth more than a dollar tomorrow. Read that again, and let it sink in for a minute.

Imagine you have a crisp one-dollar bill in your hand right now. It can be used to buy various things, like some Doritos from that vending machine or maybe a value menu item at McDonalds. Or it could also be put towards savings for a rainy day. That dollar is handy and can be put to work immediately, making your life a little better.

Now, consider the same dollar a year from now. While it's still technically a dollar, its value might not be the same. Inflation, which is the gradual rise in the cost of our everyday items and services, means that the buying power of that dollar might not stretch as far as it does today. You may find that the snack you could buy today for a dollar costs a bit more next year. It's really quite annoying and unfair, but a harsh reality that we as adults have to understand and prepare for.

This situation means that you're always in a constant battle with this irritating thing called inflation. So, does that mean you must spend all your money before it loses value? No, not necessarily. What this means is that you must make your money grow in order to keep up with inflation. We'll talk more about making your money grow using things like investing in Chapter 7. But first, let's look at how one street-smart teen handles her finances:

Meet Sarah, a high school student with a big decision to make. She's been diligently saving up for a new smartphone, and she's got $500 in her pocket. Now, let's explore two different scenarios further to understand this idea around the time value of money.

Option 1: Buy the Smartphone Now
Excited about the latest smartphone model, Sarah decides to splurge and spends her entire $500 on it. She's thrilled with her purchase and starts using it right away. The phone is lit, and she enjoys its features immediately. However, after the purchase, her savings are back to zero.

Option 2: Save and Wait
On the other hand, Sarah can consider a more patient approach. She's aware of the concept around the time value of money and the potential benefits of saving and investing. So, she thinks about putting her $500 into a savings account. She researches different

types of savings accounts and finds one that will actually pay her 5% back on her $500. Pretty cool, right? Take a mental note; we'll get more into some awesome ideas on how to make your money grow through savings in Chapter 4.

The Outcome

Option 1: Buy Now

Sarah enjoys her smartphone immediately, but she has no additional money saved. Her savings are depleted, and she's back to square one.

Option 2: Save and Wait

Sarah chooses to follow the path of delayed gratification and invests her $500. After just one year, thanks to the 5% annual return, her $500 grows to $525. Now, she not only has enough to buy the smartphone but also an extra $25 in her pocket. This bonus money could be used for phone accessories or savings for future goals.

By choosing to wait and save her money wisely, Sarah not only gets the smartphone but also has a bit of extra money to help her overall financial situation. It's a valuable lesson for teenagers and, well, anyone, really, about the benefits of being patient and making smart financial choices. It shows that a dollar saved today can grow over time, making it worth more than a dollar spent immediately. So, the next time you're faced with a financial decision, remember Sarah's story. Consider your options and try to practice the power of patience.

Scary Truths About Money

Scary truths about money? Don't fret. We're not going to talk about the financial equivalent of a horror movie. But we are going to talk about some harsh truths you need to know. The fact is some people have it harder than others. And most often, these harsh truths are not talked about. Who would want to talk about their money failures? It's usually a pretty embarrassing or shameful topic to discuss with friends, family, or peers. You see, some people, unfortunately, don't always know how to make the best financial decisions.

That's why we wrote this book. We want you to get the best financial education possible so you don't get into any of these sticky situations.

I'm going to take a minute to talk about the most common reasons people get into financial trouble. Give you some ideas on how to avoid them. And give you a sneak peek into where we will expand on each of them in the upcoming chapters. We're going to expand much more on all these topics so you will feel prepared and confident to tackle any of these common challenges.

Financial Stress
I'm sure it comes as no surprise to you that money-related stress is all too common and has serious consequences for mental and physical health. Despite working hard, some people may never achieve financial security. Think about it: constantly worrying about bills, savings, and financial security can lead to anxiety, depression, and other health issues. A good way to combat financial stress is through careful planning and turning those plans into goals. Think about the last time you made a plan or set a goal. How did it make you feel? Did you feel relief by just having a next step? Or maybe excitement at the idea of reaching that goal? It may sound cliché, but systematic and deliberate planning is the perfect antidote to financial stress. We'll dive more into this in Chapter 3.

Lack of Financial Education
We've already touched on the fact that most teenagers don't feel confident or knowledgeable on the topic of money. But would you believe me if I told you that many adults are just as lost on this topic? A lack of financial education is another scary reality. Many people aren't adequately educated about managing money, resulting in poor financial decisions and future difficulties. Like

everything in life, learning as much as you can helps you continually grow as a person. Whether that means reading books or articles, online courses, trade schools, college, or even just finding someone who you respect and look up to and picking their brain on all things money! Focusing on your education (whatever that may look like to you) is a surefire way to feel more confident with money. Throughout this book, we will offer several great resources that you can refer back to should you ever feel lost or overwhelmed. So, take notes, make scribbles, embrace Google search, but most importantly, don't forget to enjoy the process!

Unforeseen Expenses
Unexpected bills or expenses can quickly drain savings and plunge individuals or families into financial crisis. It's frightening how quickly something as unassuming as a "check engine" light can wreck someone's financial stability. So, what's the answer? Savings! The best way to fight back against unexpected expenses is to have a financial safety net in the form of savings. We will talk more about ways to save in Chapter 5. One other thing to ponder on the topic of unforeseen expenses is the power of insurance. This concept may be a foreign idea to you right now, but in Chapter 9, we'll talk about how insurance can be there when you need it most.

Debt Traps
Another scary reality is the debt trap that many individuals find themselves in. High interest rates and fees make it challenging for people to break free from the cycle of debt, whether it's loans, credit card balances, or student loans. This constant financial pressure can be incredibly stressful. That is why you must be very careful before getting into debt. While there is no need to be afraid of debt, you must be sure to avoid bad debt as much as possible. We will talk more about this in Chapters 6 and 7.

Impulse Spending
Impulse spending is another sneaky trap for your money. It's when you buy things on a whim without thinking about the

consequences. Teens and adults alike suffer from impulse spending every day. The scary truth about this is that it can quickly drain your wallet. If you remember Sarah's story and her smartphone decision, you may recall me mentioning "delayed gratification." All this means is waiting a bit before making a purchase. Doing so helps you more clearly decide if it's really worth your hard-earned cash. We'll talk more about how to conquer impulse spending in Chapter 6.

Retirement Savings Gap

A very real and scary issue is the fact that many individuals are not saving enough for retirement. The prospect of outliving one's savings can be daunting and unsettling. I know, you might be thinking, "but I'm in High School, why do I need to think about retirement?". Trust me. That is one of the most common mistakes people make. You're never too young to think about your retirement. If anything, the younger you start, the easier it will be to build a comfortable future for yourself. You'll learn more about retirement techniques in Chapter 5.

Scams and Fraud

Financial scams and fraud are unfortunately all too common nowadays. Unsuspecting individuals can fall victim to and lose significant sums of money to these schemes. Part of your responsibility as a young adult is to continue to educate yourself on this topic. Read up as much as you can to ensure you're one step ahead of fraudsters looking to steal your hard-earned cash. We'll talk more about scams and how to avoid them in Chapter 6.

Family and Relationship Strain

Money issues can be a significant source of conflicts within families and relationships. You may have experienced this yourself. Disagreements over financial matters are a leading cause of divorce and strained family ties. A good rule of thumb is to talk about money issues openly and honestly. Don't be afraid to ask questions! The idea of "getting things off your chest" can be very powerful. It can build respect and confidence and help avoid unnecessary stress.

In Chapter 10, we're going to introduce a really neat topic that will help you effectively manage challenging conversations and ways to convince others to say "YES" to your requests. Yes, you read that right. We'll talk about ways to get your parents (or anyone for that matter) to really hear you out and be more open to your ideas instead of just shutting you down with a quick "NO."

Time to Reflect

Now for some homework! No, not THAT kind of homework. Make sure you've downloaded your bonus workbook (link found on page 5) and check out the first page, titled "Journal Exercise." We'll start simple, by reflecting on and answering a few questions. Sometimes, writing things down or saying them out loud is a powerful way to discover valuable insights. It's always a great idea to start a journal, or even just a Word document, so you can revisit your answers in the future and reflect on how your money skills have grown! This exercise should give you a jumpstart.

Why is it important for you to learn more about money?
Think about your personal motivations for wanting to gain a deeper understanding of finances. Is it to find a job? Buy a car? Maybe move out of your parents' house? What drives your curiosity and need to learn more about money?

What scares you most about money?
What keeps you up at night, as it relates to money? Maybe you're worried you don't have any money? Or you have no idea where to even start? Or maybe you're afraid you don't know anything about money?

Did any of the "scary truths" which you just read about, resonate with you? Why?
We just talked about a ton of scary truths, which are very real to so many people. Did any of them hit a nerve with you? Did you think , "Oh yeah, I know all about that one"? Why do you think that was?

What would you like to gain from this book?
Just write down the first thing that comes to mind! There is no right or wrong answer here. Your first instinct is usually your best source of truth. Remember, this book is for you. In order for you to get the most from it, you have to be honest with yourself about what you want from it.

Next Up

Now that you're in the loop with money's ins and outs, are you feeling that itch to make some money? I thought so! While I'm sure learning these basics may not be the most exciting topic, having your own money is a whole different level of awesome. Onward to the next chapter, where we will explore how you can start rolling in the dough.

---

1. *Business Wire, 2022 – Survey Finds 93 of Teens Believe Financial Knowledge and Skills Are Needed to Achieve Their Life Goals*

2. *PR Newswire, 2021 – Survey finds gen z lacks knowledge and confidence in personal finance and investing*

3. *CNBC, 2022 – 54 Percent of teens feel unprepared to finance their futures survey shows*

2
Making Money - How To Get Started

M oney doesn't grow on trees. I'm sure you've heard that expression before. That's why understanding the basics of making money is a crucial skill you must master right from the start. So, let's get the ball rolling by talking about how you can roll the dough in (see what I did there?). Making cash isn't complicated, but it does require some know-how. Let me walk you through it.

The Basics of Making Money

Money—it's not just about buying cool stuff. It's your ticket to freedom. Think about it: when you've got some cash in your pocket, you probably feel like you can do what you want, when you want to. But here's the deal: it doesn't fall from the sky, and nobody's handing it out for free. That's why it's crucial to start thinking about how to earn your own money from an early age.

So, why is money so darn important? Well, it's like your passport to adulthood. It lets you take control of your life, pay for the things you need, and turn your dreams into reality. Whether it's saving up for a sweet ride, grabbing some lunch with your friends, or even thinking about funding your college education, money's got your back. And the sooner you start understanding and respecting its value, the better equipped you'll be for the future.

But how do you actually get that cash flowing? Earning money is about more than just landing a traditional 9-to-5 job. There are endless ways to rake in the dough and some are surprisingly unconventional. Think about content creation on platforms like YouTube and TikTok, selling your creative skills, freelancing, or even starting a small online business. The internet has opened up a whole new world of opportunities. You can turn your passion into a paycheck if you hustle right.

For example, if you have an entrepreneur spirit, you could start your own side hustle, like a car wash or pet-sitting service. Love crafting and DIY projects? Sell your creations online at Etsy. Or maybe you're a social media guru; you can manage accounts for local businesses. The possibilities are limitless. The point is the job market is evolving, and it's all about thinking outside the box. Embrace your creativity, and don't be afraid to explore new avenues to make that cash.

Now, let's chat about skills. Identifying your strengths and passions is like discovering your superpowers. The sooner you figure out what you're good at and what gets your heart racing, the more time you have to level up those skills. But why does that matter?

Well, my friend, the job market is constantly shifting. Some jobs that exist today might not be around in a few years, while others you have yet to hear of will become the hot new thing. So, valuable skills are your golden ticket to job security and success.

For instance, technology is advancing at lightning speed. Coding, data analysis, artificial intelligence and cybersecurity skills are all in high demand and will continue to be super relevant in the future. If you're into graphic design or video production, a world of opportunities awaits you in marketing, media, and entertainment. If you're a social media pro, you could turn your talent into a career in digital marketing or influencer marketing.

But here's the kicker: your skills can be more than just about what's hot in the job market. If you're passionate about something, go all in on it. Whether it's painting, playing an instrument, cooking, or even mastering a sport, your passion can become a source of income. Who wouldn't want to make money doing what they love?

The earlier you recognize and nurture these skills, the better. It's like planting seeds that will grow into money trees. The more you practice, learn, and improve your skills, the more valuable you become in the job market.

Remember, money is more than just pieces of paper or numbers in a bank account. It's your ticket to freedom and opportunity. Start thinking about how to earn it, explore different avenues, and identify your skills. Whether riding the wave of the digital age or turning your passions into profits, your financial future is in your hands. It's time to hustle, learn, and rake in the dough!

Finding Opportunities to Make Money

Now, we're about to drop some major truths on how to secure that bag, from snagging part-time jobs to unleashing your entrepreneurial spirit with epic side hustle ideas. Buckle up as we dive into the world of making money.

First up, part-time jobs. These are like your entry point in to the money game. But how do you find them? You can start by checking out local job listings, asking around in your community, or hitting up job search websites and apps like Indeed, Monster, or Glassdoor. Also, don't sleep on social media—sometimes job postings pop up on platforms like Facebook and LinkedIn. Always keep your eyes peeled!

But let's not stop there. It's time to think beyond the typical 9-to-5. You've got that entrepreneurial spirit, and it's time to unleash it with some creative side hustle ideas. Check these out:

- **Car Detailing.** If you're a car enthusiast with an eye for detail, offer car detailing services. People love a fresh and clean ride, and you can cash in on it!

- **Pet Sitting or Dog Walking.** Got a soft spot for fur babies? Offer pet sitting or dog walking services in your neighborhood. It's a win-win—you get to hang out with cute animals and get paid for it.

- **Tutoring.** If you excel in a particular subject or skill, become a tutor. You can help others while making some extra cash. Plus, it's a rewarding way to share your knowledge.

- **Photography Services.** Got a camera and an eye for photography? Offer your services for events like parties or take portraits of friends and family. Captured memories are always a prices treasure.

Now, let's talk about leveraging your online skills to make bank:

- **Social Media Management.** If you're a social media guru, offer your services to businesses or friends looking to up their online game. You can manage their accounts, create content, and help grow their following.

- **Side Work Apps.** Apps like Upwork or TaskRabbit are a goldmine for gig work. You can complete various tasks or odd jobs for people in your area. From running errands to assembling furniture, these apps have it all.

- **Online Surveys and Market Research.** Sign up for legit online survey sites or participate in market research studies. Your opinions matter, and you can earn some easy money by sharing them.

- **YouTube Channel.** Start your own YouTube channel if you're a social media whiz with video skills. It's a platform to share your passion, expertise, or creativity with the world. And as you grow your channel, you can make money through ads and sponsorships.

The key to making money is staying motivated and consistent. Don't expect to get rich overnight, but with determination and hustle, you can build your income steadily. The money-making world is your oyster, whether rocking a part-time job, diving into side hustles, or going digital with your skills. Get out there, get that paper, and enjoy the journey!

Networking: The Hidden Treasure

Let's talk about a serious life hack for success. Leveraging the power of connections.

Connections are like keys to doors you didn't even know existed. They open up a world of opportunities. Whether you're on the hunt for a part-time job, looking to score an internship, or even seeking advice on your dream career, the right connection can make it happen.

Imagine this: you're dreaming of becoming a graphic designer. You meet someone at a school event who's already in the industry. You chat, connect on social media, and boom! Now you've got a mentor who can offer advice or help get you in the door when you're job-hunting. That's the power of connections.

Now, let's get into your rep, your personal brand. Your reputation is like your street cred in the adult world. It's all about how people see you and what they say when you're not in the room. Building a solid personal brand can seriously boost your success.

Think about it like this: If you're known for being reliable, creative, and hardworking, people will want you on their team. So, how do you build that brand? Start by being authentic. Be you because you're awesome, just the way you are. Then, show what you're good at through your actions. Are you a problem solver? A team player? A creative genius? Let it shine, and let others see it.

Now, let's get practical with some networking tips. You can leverage school, your community, and online platforms to grow your connections and build that fantastic brand. Check out the Networking Ideas page in your bonus workbook, and try to write down some ideas of your own on how and where you can network. Here are some examples to get you started:

At school:

- **Get Involved.** Join clubs, sports, or other school activities. It's an instant way to meet like-minded people and connect over shared interests.

- **Participate in Class.** Don't be a wallflower. Speak up, ask questions, and engage with your teachers and classmates. It shows you're enthusiastic and ready to learn.

- **Volunteer.** Offer your time and skills for school events or projects. It's an amazing way to make a positive impression and give back.

In your community:

- **Attend Local Events.** Keep an eye out for local events, workshops, and gatherings. They're often packed with professionals and other teens you can connect with.

- **Volunteer in the Community.** Just like at school, community service is a win-win. You help out, and you meet great people in the process.

- **Internships and Part-Time Jobs.** Look for internships and part-time gigs in your community. It's a double win—you get experience and make connections.

Online platforms:

- **LinkedIn.** Yep, even teens can rock LinkedIn. Create a profile and connect with professionals and mentors in your field of interest.

- **Social Media.** Use your social media accounts to showcase your skills and interests. Connect with professionals and influencers in your desired industry.

- **Online Communities.** Join online forums, groups, and communities related to your interests. It's a goldmine for making connections and learning from others.

Networking isn't just about what others can do for you—it's about how you can help each other. Be genuine, follow up with people, and be a good friend first. You never know where those connections will take you.

There's a world of endless opportunities driven by who you know and how you present yourself. So, get out there, meet cool peeps, and build that killer personal brand. Your future self will thank you!

Putting Pen to Paper

Let's take a moment to reflect and get those wheels turning about some job and money-making ideas. Use the Job Ideas template in the bonus workbook, to start journaling areas that pique your interest. It could be anything, from starting your own clothing brand to becoming a social media influencer or even launching a food truck. The sky's the limit.

Try to start with why these ideas get you fired up! Write down the reasons, and let's dig deeper:

- **Interests & Passions.** What sets your heart on fire about this idea? Is it something you genuinely love to do? Maybe you adore fashion and dream of designing your own clothes. Or you're a foodie who wants to share your love for cooking with the world.

- **Skills.** Do you have some skills that make you a rock star in this area? Maybe you're a cosmetic queen and could be the next hot makeup artist. Or a natural at public speaking and think you could inspire and educate others.

- **Impact.** Think about how your idea could make a difference. Is it about making people's lives easier, entertaining them, or solving problems? Imagine the positive impact you could have on others and write it down.

- **Money.** Let's keep it real; moolah matters. Does this idea have the potential to bring in some cash? You don't have to be a money-grabber, but you want to ensure your passion project can support your lifestyle.

- **Career Ideas.** After thinking about and writing down your ideas, does it translate into anything specific regarding a career? If not, that's ok! Pro-tip: You can always use Google to do research on how your interests, passions, and skills might align with specific careers.

There are no wrong answers here. Your ideas are like seeds and this exercise is about nurturing them. So, what did you come up with? It's time to explore, experiment, and see which one takes you to the next level.

Now that you've written down those ideas and why they excite you, could you take a moment to prioritize them? Which one gives you the most adrenaline rush? Which one aligns best with your values and goals? That's the idea you should seriously consider pursuing.

This is all about exploration. Start small, test the waters, and see how it feels. Talk to people who are already in the game and get their insights. Keep the ideas simmering on the back burner while you learn and grow.

Are you ready to take the first step towards one of those ideas? It could be as simple as doing some online research, applying for a job, or reaching out to a mentor in that field. The most important thing is to start somewhere.

Don't Forget to Put Your Best Foot Forward

When you're applying for part-time jobs, it's important to put your best foot forward. Crafting a killer resume highlighting your skills, experience, and any volunteer work or extracurricular activities, can really set you apart from others. Even with little job experience, you can showcase your reliability, teamwork, and dedication. You can even include a creative cover letter explaining why you want the job to show your enthusiasm for the position. When you land that interview, be punctual, dress the part, and come prepared with thoughtful questions. Confidence is key! And don't forget to check out Chapter 10, where I unveil the secrets to getting a "YES". These techniques can be applied to many things in life, but more specifically to a job interview.

Writing a resume can be overwhelming, but you don't need to overthink it. Employers will know you're a teenager and won't be expecting a fancy resume packed with "experience." The fact that you took time and put effort into composing a resume will likely make you stand out from other applicants. We've included a couple of simple resume templates in your bonus workbook to reference as a starting point. Take a look at page 5 and 6 of the workbook, and start thinking about what you can bring to the table for future employers!

Next Up

Now that you have some ideas on how to stack up some cash, what comes next? Well, making money is just the beginning of your financial journey. It's like being a baker – you wouldn't just whip up some cookies without a recipe, right? In the same way, you shouldn't earn money without a clear plan for how to use it.

Think about it this way: imagine you're baking that batch of cookies. You put in all the time and effort, and they come out perfectly. But what's the point if you let those cookies go stale or make more than you can eat? It's the same with your hard-earned cash. You've got to have a plan.

Welcome to the world of goal-setting. Consider goals like your recipes for financial success. Whether saving up for the latest gaming console, planning a dinner date with that special someone, or securing that 'dough' for college, knowing how to manage expectations for your money is critical. Remember that financial success isn't about having stacks of cash; it's about having control over your money and ultimately using it to reach your goals.

Having a plan, setting goals, and executing those goals puts you in the driver's seat of your financial future. In the next chapter, we will talk about how you can keep rocking the money-making path by taking full advantage of goal setting. And don't worry, it's not as complicated as it might seem… when you know how to do it right. See you there!

3

Ready, Set, Goal

H ave you ever been stuck a "fear of missing out" funk? Watching your friends rock the latest gear or hitting up epic hotspots while you're stuck scrolling in agony? In this chapter, we'll focus on hitting the brakes on that pity party and turning the table. It's not rocket science – it just takes a sprinkle of planning magic. Make the right moves, and soon your crew will be like, "Hold up, how'd you pull that off?!"

This chapter reveals how fear of missing out can be a powerful motivator to get you planning your goals like a boss. By the time we're done here, you'll feel so confident you won't ever have to worry about missing out again. You'll learn how to create and set attainable goals, ensuring you achieve them faster than you thought possible.

Setting Savings Goals

Here's the deal – when you set a savings goal, it's like giving your money a mission, a purpose. And guess what? That purpose makes saving way more exciting and rewarding.

Now, let's get into the nitty-gritty of the psychology behind it. Having a clear target triggers something in your brain – it's like a savings superpower. The benefits? Just the thrill of accomplishment and the sweet taste of success. When you hit that goal, it's a victory dance kind of moment.

Start with short-term goals. Think of instant gratification, like saving for that new game or concert ticket. It's the blink-and-you'll-be-there kind of goal. It is, however, important to be careful with short-term goals. These goals aren't always super-mega-critical. It's certainly okay to treat yourself once in a while, but remember to stay focused. Spending too much on non-essentials can leave a hole in your bank account. And you may find yourself struggling to find the cash for the things you really need.

How about those medium-term goals? We're talking about the good stuff, like a new phone or laptop. Things that may take several months to save up for. Dreaming of a road trip? Break down that $500 goal into $42 monthly slices, and you're on the money. Other medium-term goals might be things like college expenses – books, classes, the whole shebang. So, figure out the costs, focus on saving up, and trust me, you'll feel like a boss once you have the cash for those goodies.

Now let's focus on a crucial point: long-term goals. We're running a marathon here. Long-term goals could be buying a car or saving for an apartment. Break down that $5,000 ride into $140 monthly pit stops. After a few years, you'll be ready to go check out the dealerships. It's the slow and steady win-the-race type of vibe. As the name suggests, long-term goals are things you can't save for in weeks or months. It might take several years, to get the cash you need to pay for this stuff. That's why breaking down your big goal into smaller bits helps you stay on track. Think about it: marathon runners never think about running 26 miles. They focus on running one mile at a time. I know everyone says that. But believe me. Approaching goals in smaller, organized chunks can help avoid feeling like it's too much to handle.

Practice Makes Perfect

Setting goals may feel overwhelming at first, but remember, everyone has to start somewhere, right? You can't expect to make your dreams come true overnight. You will need to work at it. Think about it this way: no one gets a million subscribers on the first day they open their Insta profile. It takes time and effort to build a loyal following.

So, be ready to work on building your goal-setting techniques. And before you know it, you'll have the skills to play the game of life in all-star mode. Think about how hard your favorite game was when you started. As you continued to practice and play, did the game become easier?

That's how goal-setting works. Stay focused and consistent and you'll soon turn your money game into a boss-level adventure.

SMART Goals for the Win

It's time to unravel the mystery of turning dreams into concrete goals with the ultimate weapon in goal-setting: the SMART technique. It's like our secret code to transform wishful thinking into an action-packed roadmap. Let's look at how to execute these techniques:

Specific -
Setting goals is like choosing a destination for your next big adventure. It's about being clear and precise. When you set a goal, it's time to ditch the vague and embrace the laser-focused. Instead of a general "do better in school," aim for "get a B or higher in math this semester." Specific goals are like setting the exact location on your GPS and guiding you to where you want to go without any detours.

Measurable -
Goals need to be as concrete as the score in a video game. They should be something you can track and measure. Change "save money" to "save $500 for a new laptop." This way, you have a clear target to hit, and you'll know exactly when you've achieved it, making your goal a tangible victory.

Achievable -
Your goals should be like advancing in a game – challenging but definitely possible. If "starting a YouTube channel" feels too big, begin with "upload one video each week." Break down your larger ambitions into smaller, manageable tasks that you can tackle and win.

Relevant -
Your goals should match your current priorities and be relevant to your overall storyline. Think of them as the critical tests that determine your GPA in life. If you're caught up in planning the ultimate summer road trip, yet your real task is to ace an exam for a scholarship, it may be time to realign your focus. Remember, your goals should directly contribute to your bigger picture, keeping you on track with what's most important to you.

Time-Bound -
Goals should have a deadline, like finishing a project before the school break. This adds a sense of urgency and helps you prioritize. Instead of a vague goal like "learn to code," set a deadline, such as "complete an online coding course by the end of the semester."

Time-bound goals keep you focused and motivated, turning your aspirations into actions with a clear finish line.

SMART Goals in Action

Now that you have an idea of what SMART goals are, let's put them into action. Use the SMART goals template in your bonus workbook, to write down some goals that align with the SMART approach. Here are some examples that will set you off in the right direction:

Specific

- A *Vague* **Example of a Specific Goal May Be:** "Take that special someone on the perfect date."

- **Whereas a *SMART* Example of a Specific Goal is:** "Save $100 over the next month to go to dinner and a movie, by setting aside $25 from my weekly allowance."

Measurable

- A *Vague* **Example of a Measurable Goal May Be:** "Make some extra cash."

- **Whereas a *SMART* Example of a Measurable Goal Is:** "Earn $150 in the next two months by offering dog-walking services every weekend at $15 per walk. Keep track of my earnings every week."

Achievable

- A *Vague* **Example of an Achievable Goal May Be:** "Become a millionaire."

- **Whereas a *SMART* Example of an Achievable Goal Is:** "Save $500 by the end of the school year by cutting back on eating out and contributing $20 per week to my savings. This will help me learn to manage money and build a solid financial foundation."

Relevant

- **A *Vague* Example of a Relevant Goal May Be**: "Save some money in a random bank account."

- **Whereas A *SMART* Example of a Relevant Goal Is:** "Save $200 in a savings account by the end of the year, aligning with my plans to save money for a specific goal such as upgrading my phone or computer."

Time-Bound

- **A *Vague* Example of a Time-Bound Goal May Be**: "Learn to budget."

- **Whereas a *SMART* Example of a Time-Bound Goal Is:** "Create a monthly budgeting plan by the start of the next school semester, breaking down expenses and setting aside $30 a month for savings. This will help me develop practical money management habits within the next three months."

Remember: These goals must make sense for you. You can only expect to make things happen by adjusting your sights to your specific needs and wants. So, make sure to keep your eyes the prize!

Don't Let FOMO Hold You Back

FOMO, or Fear of Missing Out, is the gut punch you get when the gang's out there living their best lives, and you're stuck feeling left out. It can be a tough pill to swallow. But what if you could turn that FOMO into a powerful motivator to propel you towards your goals? It may be hard to believe, but let's break down it down. Because who says FOMO can't be the kick in the pants you need to level up?

- **Social Media as an Amplifier.** Nowadays social media is the ultimate FOMO megaphone. You're scrolling, double-tapping, and BAM! Everyone's flexing their epic lives, leaving you drowning in FOMO vibes. It's like a highlight reel of everyone else's awesomeness, and suddenly, your life feels a bit meh.

- **Turning FOMO into Rocket Fuel.** But guess what? FOMO isn't the enemy; it's your sidekick in disguise. You can use that FOMO as rocket fuel for your goals. See that friend with the killer skateboard? Instead of moping about it, let it light a fire under you, to save up for *your* dream board.

- **Goal-Setting Magic.** First step: pinpoint what triggers your feeling of missing out. What's making you feel so envious or left out? The latest gadgets? Trendy clothes? Epic vacations? Cool. Now, turn those triggers into your goal-setting playground.

- **Set SMART Goals.** Remember our SMART goals? Specific, Measurable, Achievable, Relevant, and Time-Bound. Apply those methods. If FOMO's got you craving the latest Sephora product, set a goal to save up for it. Make it specific – like "save $100 for my Sephora trip in two months." You see what did there? You just turned FOMO into your financial co-pilot.

- **Finding Motivation.** Let FOMO be the kick that propels you into action. Turn jealousy into motivation and scroll with a mission. See someone driving your dream car? Instead of drowning in FOMO tears, let it be the spark to plan and save for your dream ride.

As you can see, your fear of missing out is not your nemesis; it's your secret weapon. Embrace it, set those killer goals, and watch your FOMO transform into a launchpad for success.

The Joy of Missing Out... Say What?!

Okay, so we've talked about FOMO. But have you ever heard of the term "JOMO?" Enter JOMO – the Joy of Missing Out. Yes, there is such a thing as finding joy in missing out! That's right: we're flipping the script on FOMO and turning it into a celebration of doing you. How can you embrace the JOMO lifestyle, where missing out isn't a loss but a strategic move? Here's the deal:

- **JOMO 101.** JOMO, or the Joy of Missing Out, involves feeling happy and satisfied about missing out on something. JOMO consists of feeling content with sitting on the sidelines rather than feeling anxious or envious about missing out on things. The key to JOMO lies in ditching unnecessary stuff while focusing on what truly matters in your life.

- **The Benefits of Opting Out.** Think about it – by opting out on occasion, you're not just saving your time and energy, you're also protecting your hard-earned cash. It's a strategic power move that turns those moments of "man, I wish I could have been there"... Into a proud moment of "wow, look how much I've saved!"

- **The JOMO Lifestyle Hack.** Recognize how much power there is in saying 'no' when needed. Instead of chasing every event or impulse purchase, embrace the JOMO lifestyle. Skip that expensive concert and rock out to your favorite tunes at home. Pass on the latest fashion craze and focus on improving your finances instead.

- **The Nest Egg Effect.** JOMO isn't just about missing out; it's about gaining control. Every time you opt out of a splurge, it's a deposit into your nest egg – that sweet financial cushion that screams independence. Picture this: while others are blowing cash, you're building a fortress of financial freedom.

- **Celebrate the Wins.** Turn missing out into a victory dance. Celebrate the fact that you're making conscious choices for your future. While others are caught up in the FOMO frenzy, you're sipping on the JOMO juice, knowing that every smart decision is a step closer to your financial goals.

Ultimately, FOMO and JOMO are not evil villains. They may look mean, but they're precisely what you need to get off the couch and turn your dream financial future into a reality.

The Vision Board Hack

It's time to dive into the ultimate cool-kid activity: creating a vision board. Trust me, it's like Instagram for your dreams but way more personal. Get ready to turn your financial goals into a visual masterpiece that'll have you motivated AF. Print out the Vision Board template in your bonus workbook, or just buy a poster board at your local crafts store and try to unleash your creativity. Let your dreams take center stage. Your vision board is more than just a neat piece of art. It's a roadmap to your financial awesomeness.

Here's your step-by-step guide:

- **What's a Vision Board Anyway?** Think of it as a DIY dream gallery. It's a place where your goals get a spotlight, and you get to curate the vibe of your future. Cut out pics from magazines, print stuff from the web – whatever screams YOUR goals.

- **Visualize Your Dreams.** Close your eyes and picture your dream life. Financial freedom, travel, epic gadgets – the whole nine yards. Now, find images that match those dreams. If you're saving for a dream trip, slap on pics of your dream destination. It's like building a personal vision playlist.

- **Gather Your Materials.** First things first, let's gather the essentials. Get your hands on magazines, newspapers, or any visual materials you can cut up or print out. You'll also need scissors, glue, a large board or poster paper, and markers or pens. This is about letting your creativity flow, so don't be shy about including sketches, symbols, or anything else that speaks to you.

- **Cut, Paste, Slay.** Get hands-on, literally. Cut out those dreamy images and paste them on your board. Use colors, quotes, and anything that resonates with your vibe. This board is a visual representation of your financial goals, so let it scream 'YOU.'

- **Focus on the Feels.** Each image should spark an emotion. If it's a picture of that dream car, you should feel the thrill of cruising with the wind in your hair. If it's a beach vacay, feel the sand between your toes. Your vision board isn't just a pretty collage; it's a feels trip to your future success.

- **Arrange and Glue.** Once you have a delightful collection of images, arrange them on your board in a way that feels visually appealing and meaningful to you. This isn't about perfection; it's about personal connection. When you're satisfied with the arrangement, glue everything down.

- **Make It Visible.** This shouldn't be a hidden treasure – display that board where you'll see it daily. Bedroom wall, study desk, or even the fridge – wherever you'll catch those vibes. It's not just about creating; it's about living your goals daily.

- **Update and Upgrade.** Your goals aren't stagnant, and neither is your vision board. Keep updating it as your dreams evolve. New goals? Swap in new pics. Achieved something? Celebrate by adding a victory image. It's a living, breathing masterpiece.

- **Share the Vision.** Let your squad in on the action. Share your vision board vibes. Who knows, maybe you'll inspire them to craft their own. It's like starting a vision board revolution, one friend at a time.

Next Up

Alrighty, you've got your goals all mapped out – the dream rides, the tech upgrades, the epic adventures. Now, let's kick it into gear and talk about how to make those dreams a reality.

Think of it this way; goal setting is like planning your ultimate road trip. But a roadmap won't drive the car for you. That's where budgeting swoops in as your slick, personal GPS. Imagine you're cruising through the twists and turns of income, dodging the potholes of expenses, and occasionally hitting that financial speed bump. Budgeting is your co-pilot, keeping you on track to reach those goal destinations.

Now, I know budgeting might sound like the party pooper of finance, but hear me out. It's not about slamming on the brakes; it's about taking the wheel and steering your money towards what truly matters. That new gaming console? Budget for it. That new outfit? Budget for it. You're not cutting out the fun; you're just setting the stage for financial wins.

So, are you ready to boss up those bucks? Then let's roll on!

Before we move on to the next chapter, here's a fun exercise to see what you've learned thus far. Can you answer the questions and complete the Crossword Puzzle? If you need a hand, the answer key can be found at the end of the book.

Down:

1. A platform where you can make videos on, as a side-hustle
2. Buying something without planning
3. Type of goal that is possible or within reach
7. Regularly setting aside money
8. Acronym for feeling happy about missing out
10. A job involving teaching others a specific skill or subject

Across:

4. Type of goal that is clear and detailed
5. To build professional relationships for career opportunities
6. A charge or cost for something
9. A gradual increase in prices over time

4

Budget Like a Boss

Ready to give your money skills a serious boost? Think of your cash as your own personal team, and you're the one calling the shots. We're here to give you the lowdown on how to make your money stick with you through thick and thin. Whether you're saving up for that trendy new product or eyeing a sweet set of wheels, we've got the tips to keep your dreams and your bank account on the same page.

Remember, it's not just about stacking cash; it's about getting your money to work as hard as you do. In this chapter, we'll break down everything you need to know to perfect your budgeting game and take charge of your finances.

Nail Budgeting Basics

Alright, let's simplify budgeting in a way that even your Grandma would give it a thumbs up.

Knowing Your Income

Knowing your income is like knowing the amount of fuel in your car's tank; it tells you how far you can go with your budgeting journey. Simply put, your income is the money you earn. The paycheck you pull in from your part-time job, the cash you make from that side hustle like dog walking, or even the allowance you get for doing chores. It's all considered your income and every penny counts. It's about understanding what you have to work with so you can plan for the essentials or save up for a rainy day, and still have some left-over for the fun stuff. Getting a clear picture of your income is an important first step to taking control of your money and avoiding the stress of overspending.

Budgeting to the Rescue

Think of your budget as the roadmap for all those hard-earned bucks. Got $200 in the bank? Your budget is the captain steering the ship, helping you decide the fate of each dollar. Eyeing a new pair of fresh kicks? Saving up for the latest skincare product? Wanting to put aside some cash for a rainy day? Budget's got you. It's like having a sidekick that's making sure you don't blow your cash on stuff you don't really need or can't afford. Or in other words, your guardian angel against impulse buys and shiny distractions.

Enter the epic battle of Needs versus Wants.

Let's say you need to do some back-to-school shopping and you have $100 to spend. You immediately set your sights on that designer backpack that's shouting your name. But, you also need to snag the essentials – school supplies, fresh threads, maybe a new book. Budget's the referee in this showdown, helping you strike the right balance. Maybe you compromise on the backpack and go for a stylish yet budget-friendly option so you can still rock the halls with your essentials intact.

Or perhaps you're drooling over a new pair of Beats headphones. They're sleek, they're loud, perfect for jamming out. But, you're also saving up for prom. Which obviously is going to be the best-night-ever. Cue the mental tug-of-war. Budget steps in for a reality check, tapping you on the shoulder, saying, "Hold up, young grasshopper, balance is the key." Maybe you should hold off on the headphones for now or scout for alternatives? Like some second-hand options or another brand that's less harsh on your wallet. You've got to make sure you're decked out for prom, right? And ensure you have all the epic essentials to make it legendary. After all, those headphones aren't going anywhere, but prom night? That's a once-in-a-lifetime event, that'll turn into a memory you'll replay forever.

Remember, in the budgeting world, it's not about shutting down your wants – we're not here for that. It's about empowering you to make informed decisions and leveling up to be a savvy boss of your finances.

The Name of the Game is "Budget"

Let's debunk the myth that budgets are out to spoil our fun. It's actually quite the opposite. Budgets aren't here to cramp your style. They're all about unlocking that independence you've been craving. Your ticket to the freedom zone. So where do we start?

You can start with short-term fun, like snagging concert tickets or a fancy dinner. A budget can help you allocate a chunk of your cash specifically for these moments. It's not about saying no to the good times but saying, "Hey, I got this much for the concert. Let's make it legendary."

Then you've got long-term goals, like gearing up for college or cruising in that dream ride. They'll also need a slice of the budget pie. Crafting a budget means you can save up for these major milestones, without sacrificing day-to-day fun.

And finally there's the "rainy days" fund. Which I'm sure sounds as exciting as watching paint dry. But trust me, life can throw some curveballs. Unexpected expenses or surprise opportunities can pop-up at any moment. Having that rainy day fund is like having a financial umbrella. Boring now, lifesaver later.

If you're serious about becoming a budgeting ninja but keeping the fun alive, embrace the concepts taught in this chapter. When you plan for the future, you'll be ready for whatever life throws at you.

50/30/20 Rule: A Simple Formula for Success

The 50/30/20 rule is a clear and effective method for organizing your finances. Here's how it works: allocate 50% of your income to essential needs, 30% to personal wants, and 20% towards savings or debt repayment.

- **50% for Needs:** This portion covers the basics, such as transportation, gas, school essentials, or food. These are the expenses necessary for daily living.

- **30% for Wants:** This is the fun part of your budget. Money set aside for things that bring you joy but aren't essential for survival. It could include shopping sprees, hobbies, entertainment, or other fun activities.

- **20% for Savings:** The final slice is dedicated to building your financial future. This includes saving for emergencies, investing for long-term goals, or paying down debt.

The beauty of the 50/30/20 rule is its flexibility. It gives you a solid starting point to handle your cash, but it's also about adjusting the numbers to best fit your lifestyle and financial goals. Wanna save up a more quickly and cut back on the splurges? Go for it. Or maybe you need to spend a bit more on your must-haves – that's fine too. The goal is to find that sweet spot that keeps you happy today, while keeping your future finances in check.

The 50/30/20 Rule in Action

All right, let's break down the 50/30/20 rule with a real-life teen twist.

We'll start with the 50% squad – your needs—the real-world essentials. Think school supplies, maybe chipping in for gas or bus fare to keep you rolling to those weekend hangouts. Let's say you're bringing in $200 a month from your part-time job. You would put $100 (50%) towards these needs. This chunk of your income goes towards the foundation that keeps your teen empire standing tall.

Next up, the 30% crew – your wants. The fuel for the fun. Thinking of an unforgettable date night? You've got 30% or your original $200 paycheck, to make it happen. That's $60, at your disposal. This is your chance to splurge a bit on the things light up your world. Think of it as your all-access pass to the fun parts of being a teenager, where you get to spend smart and enjoy big.

And last but not least, the 20% dream team – your savings. The last 20% slice of your paycheck, can be tucked away nicely into your savings account. Whether it's the emergency fund for that phone that decides to play dead or a reserve for future road trips with friends, this portion is your ticket to fun adventures and financial safety nets, ensuring you're prepared for both the unexpected and the exciting plans ahead.

Again, the 50/30/20 rule isn't etched in stone. It's your canvas to paint on. If you're feeling more frugal, tweak those percentages. Maybe go 60/25/15 or 40/35/25. It's all about what suits your vibe.

If you're looking for a helping hand, check out the cool financial calculator from NerdWallet. It's much easier to get started with budgeting when you have a neat tool like this at your fingertips! Budgeting calculators help you quickly figure out how to adjust your numbers to align with your financial goals.

Staying on Track

Let's take a moment to talk about a crucial part of your financial journey: Staying on track. It does take some discipline and commitment, but if done correctly it can elevate your money management skills to expert status.

- First up, tracking your expenses. Think of it as giving your cash a social media account where every dollar posts its whereabouts. It might sound tedious, but it's the key to unveiling where your funds are flowing. You can use apps, spreadsheets, or just write it down in a handy notebook – pick your weapon and track away.

- Next up, reviewing your budget regularly. It's not a one-time deal or a set-it-and-forget-it approach. Regular check-ins allow you to gauge whether you're still on track or if you might need to recalibrate your strategy. Life changes, right? Well, so should your budget. Maybe that part-time gig turned into a full-blown hustle. Or maybe some surprise expenses have showed up. This dynamic approach ensures your budget keeps up with whatever life throws at you, making it easier to handle your money with confidence.

- And last but not least, setting realistic goals. Sure, we all dream of becoming money moguls, but remember to keep it real. Break down those big dreams into bite-sized, achievable goals. Just as we discussed in the last chapter, having achievable goals not only keeps you motivated but also on the right track. Think of it as your financial bucket list. And make sure to celebrate the small wins on your journey to the big victories.

Now let's break down each of these topics a bit further.

Tracking Expenses

Tracking expenses is like having a secret weapon to conquer the money maze. No matter how small your cash flow is, you want to keep tabs on it.

- Start with some old-school vibes. Grab a simple notebook. Think of it as your financial diary, where every buck gets its own page. Jot down what you spent, where you spent it, and why. It's like giving your money a voice – let it spill its secrets.

- Now, for the tech-savvy crew, we've got budgeting apps like Mint (now merged with CreditKarma) or PocketGuard. Connect your accounts, and they'll do all the heavy lifting for you. You can categorize your spending, create custom budgets, and even set alerts to notify you if you're getting a little too spend-happy. It's budgeting in the 21st century – slick, easy, and convenient.

Whether scribbling in a notebook or tapping away on your phone, the key is to track every move your money makes. Those little expenses? They add up like puzzle pieces, forming a bigger financial picture. So grab your tool of choice – be it a notebook or your favorite app – and start tracking like the money ninja you were born to be. Your budget will thank you later.

Keep an Eye on Stuff

Now let's talk about why making a habit of checking in regularly with your budget, is important. Think of it like tuning up your favorite playlist – it's all about keeping those money vibes in sync.

- First, the golden rule is to review your budget at least once a month. Life moves fast, and so does your cash flow. Maybe that part-time gig turned into a money-making machine, or all that weekend fun is taking a toll on your budget. Be sure to keep your budget fresh, by periodically checking in and updating it as needed.

- Regular check-ins of your budget help you understand whether you're staying on track or if you've veered off course. This process isn't just about identifying mistakes; it's about actively managing your finances. For example, if you notice your spending on snacks has increased significantly, you might need to make some adjustments. Alternatively, if you've been super on-point with your budget, perhaps it's time to reward yourself with a little something extra.

Don't think of it as a chore. Think of it as a financial power move. It's about staying ahead of the game and ensuring your budget reflects your current reality. And hey, who knows? You might spot some trends, find ways to save more, or even discover some extra cash for that next adventure.

Keep It Real

Remember to be as realistic with your budget as you are with your Instagram captions. We're talking about setting epic but *achievable* goals that won't leave you eating instant noodles for a month.

First rule of thumb: don't aim for the financial moon if you're just starting your journey. Setting sky-high savings goals might sound tempting, but should be a no-go if they leave you skipping meals or cutting down on the essentials. We're all about improving but without the burden of added stress.

So be sure to start small, like mini-road-trip-small. Set achievable savings goals that won't make you want to pull your hair out. It's like going to the gym – you don't start with lifting a car; you start with the weights you can handle.

Why? Because we're in it for the long game. Gradually increase those savings vibes over time. It's like building a fortress, one brick at a time. Maybe this month, it's saving up for that concert ticket. Next month, it's adding a little more to your emergency fund. Slow and steady wins the financial race.

Remember, it's not about flexing unrealistic goals; it's about creating a budget that becomes your financial best friend. So, keep it real, set goals that match your hustle, and watch your savings grow without the stress.

Budgeting Cheat Sheet

Be sure to check out Page 10 of your bonus workbook, for a helpful budgeting cheat sheet. It offers some common terminology and definitions, awesome apps you may want to consider downloading and a visual reminder of the 50/30/20 rule, which you can reference at any time!

Budgeting In Action

Ready to set up your first budget? Use the handy monthly budget planner in your bonus workbook, to get you started!

Step 1: Know Your Income

List all the sources of money flowing into your life. It could be that part-time job at Burger King, the weekly allowance from your folks, dog-walking for your neighbor, or the dollars rolling in from selling your vintage games on eBay. However you're pulling in some extra cash, write it down. It's important to clearly understand your starting point.

Step 2: List Your Expenses

Now let's spill the tea on where your money's going. First, list your essentials and needs. The fuel that keeps you going, like gas, school supplies or food. Next, be sure to track your wants. The things that add some flavor to your life, like Netflix or H&M finds. Don't be shy – every dollar gets its moment in the spotlight.

Step 3: Plan Your Savings

Lastly, choose a set amount or follow the 50/30/20 rule, and dedicate it towards your savings vault. It's your call. But remember, this step isn't just about socking away money, it's about laying the groundwork for your future aspirations. Whether it's saving for a concert, a new gadget, or just a rainy day, having a plan puts you in the driver's seat.

Choose Your Own Adventure

Think of your budget as the ultimate "Choose Your Own Adventure" book for your finances. It doesn't *have* to be a boring story that puts you to sleep. You can turn it into your own page-turning adventure that unfolds based on your decisions. Life throws curveballs and opportunities alike, and with each new chapter, you might find a surprise bonus waiting for you. Your budget is the guidebook that helps you navigate these choices, ensuring each decision aligns with the evolving plot of your money journey. Just like in those books, every choice leads to new possibilities, and your budget empowers you to steer those stories toward your ultimate ending.

Next Up

Are you feeling empowered yet? You should be!

Let's spice things up a bit. What if I told you your current saving method might be cramping your style and holding you back from financial greatness? Intrigued much?

It's time to turn into financial detectives to uncover hidden obstacles and elevate your savings game. The truth is, you may need to break free from old habits to uncover a more profitable approach. In the next chapter we'll explore why your savings stash may actually be *costing* you money.

5

That Saving Stash May Be Costing You Money

L et's now reflect and take a page from a celebrity money game. Selena Gomez dropped some serious wisdom in her chat with WSJ Magazine, preaching about the real deal. She reminds us, "It's crucial that we get a real understanding of the importance of saving, investing, and planning for our future." But what if your stash in that piggy bank is low-key sabotaging your financial game? Hoarding cash under your mattress might feel safe, but there's a smarter way to handle your money. Imagine putting those dollars to work, actively helping you chase your dreams instead of just lying there idle.

So, get ready to flip that piggy bank upside down and make every dollar pop. In this chapter we dive into how to prepare for your future financial success.

Are My Savings Too Basic?

Saving money is just saving money, right? Should be pretty simple? Well, it turns out that saving money isn't quite that simple. Yes, you can stash your cash in a jar somewhere. But if you're not careful, you might actually *lose* money. Say what?!

The Mattress Myth

Let's kick it off by talking about the "mattress myth." There are several key reasons why stashing your cash under your mattress could be a classic lousy money move. Here's why:

First off, inflation is like that sneaky villain in your financial story. It's why your grandma could buy a burger for a nickel, but now you're dropping serious bucks for the same thing. Prices keep climbing, but if your money is chilling' under the mattress, it's basically stuck in a time warp, not growing, not hustling.

Picture this: you're saving up for the ultimate gaming setup or that new iPhone. If your money isn't out there working hard for you, it's losing its value over time. You worked hard for that money; the least it can do is return the favor, right? Remember, inflation is always doing its thing, prices are skyrocketing, and your cash is constantly playing catch-up.

Now, imagine if your money was out there, fighting inflation and flexing its own growth game. Your money needs to evolve and grow faster than prices rise to outpace inflation, so you're not left in the dust.

Here's the bottom line: The mattress myth is like trying to win a gaming tournament with a basic setup—it's just not going to cut it. It's time to break free, make smarter decisions, and let that money hustle as hard as you do.

The Magic of Compound Interest

Compound interest isn't like the basic, one-time kind of interest. It's more like a snowball rolling downhill – it keeps getting bigger as it adds more and more to itself over time. Imagine you drop some bucks into a high-interest savings account. In the first round, you earn interest on your initial deposit. Now, in round two, you're not just earning interest on what you put in—you're earning interest on the total sum of your account, including the interest from round one. It's "compounding" and continuing to accumulate, growing and doing its thing like a financial superhero.

The longer your money chills in the right investment, the crazier this compound interest party gets. Your money can be out there making its own money, and over time, it's not just a side hustle; it becomes a full-blown money empire.

Here's the best part: the sooner you start, the longer your money has to compound. That's why time is on your side in the compound interest game. Don't be afraid to take the leap and let your money work for you!

Saving with a Purpose

Let's talk about saving with a purpose because, let's be real, just stashing away cash for the heck of it is so last season. We're all about those intentional money moves, and here's how:

The first step is to set clear goals. Remember, goals are like giving your money a roadmap. Whether scoring that vintage collectible, jetting off to Coachella, or building an emergency fund, giving your money a purpose helps it go the extra mile for you.

Think about it this way: You're on a mission to upgrade your sneaker game. You set a goal to cop those limited-edition kicks in, let's say, six months. Now you've got a deadline, a finish line to hustle toward.

It's not just about saving; it's a game plan to ensure you're rocking those fresh kicks on your timeline.

Goals also bring that extra dose of motivation. Instead of mindlessly tossing coins into a jar, imagine being fueled by the excitement of getting closer to what you want. It's like your personal financial cheer team, rooting you on you every step of the way.

Where does that bring us? No more wandering in the money maze, wondering what's what. It's all laid out—where you're headed, when you'll get there, and the exact steps to make it happen.

Always remember that having a purpose is the best way to keep your money game on track!

Where to Park Your Money

We know it's important to save money. But now the question is: where? Let's get into some deets on where you can park your money so you're covered no matter what.

Know Where to Stash

So where should you *really* park that hard-earned money? Start thinking about banks, online platforms, and efficient savings accounts. Here's the 411 on choosing the right spot to stash your cash:

- **Banks.** Your neighborhood bank is like the original gangster. It's familiar; you can walk in and chat with the bank guy or gal (who are also known as a "teller"), and maybe they'll toss in a lollipop. But, the interest rates at these banks can be as thrilling as watching grass grow. Traditional banks are like the tortoises of the savings game—steady but not breaking any speed records.

- **Online Platforms.** Enter the cool kids on the block. Online platforms are like the disruptors, usually offering better interest rates than your local bank. They're all about modern apps, no lines, and no paper trails. Just tap, swipe, and watch your money grow. Plus, they often have lower fees, so more cash stays in your pocket.

- **High-Yield Savings.** Now, this is where things heat up. High-yield savings accounts are like the rockstars of the savings world. They offer higher interest rates than both traditional banks and online platforms. It's like getting an A-lister treatment for your money. But some do have minimum balance requirements or withdrawal restrictions, so be sure to read the fine print.

Choosing the right spot for your cash is crucial. It's not just about the interest rates; it's about what fits your vibe. Need that in-person connection? A traditional bank might be for you. Living the tech-savvy life? Online platforms could be a better fit. Eager to see your money grow quickly? Say hello to high-yield savings accounts.

Diversify to Multiply

Now it's time to focus on spicing up your saving game. It's not just about tossing cash into a basic bank account—it's about leveling up with some financial flavor. Enter the world of diversification, where your money gets a private pass to different venues like CDs and Money Market Accounts. Here's the lowdown:

- **Basic Bank Accounts.** As I mentioned, they're the OG, like your favorite comfort food. Easy to use and familiar, but in reality, the interest rates are kind of a snooze fest. Your money's just chilling there, not exactly breaking a sweat.

- **CDs (Certificates of Deposit).** Imagine your money going to a financial party where it hangs out for a set period time, and in return, it gets a VIP-level interest rate. That's like a certificate of deposit. The catch with CDs is that you must lock in your money for a specific period, typically 6, 12 or 24 months. And when it's time to bounce, you cash out with extra money. It's more of a commitment, but who says commitment has to be a bad thing?

- **High-Yield Savings Accounts.** As mentioned before, high-yield savings accounts are a great place to start. They often offer higher than average interest rates but may come with certain restrictions or requirements, such as minimum deposits or minimum monthly balances. It's like upgrading from a slow, steady walk to a sprint; your money works harder and faster, accumulating more interest.

- **Money Market Accounts.** Think of these as the hybrid between a high-yield savings account and a CD. They offer better interest rates than your regular bank account, but you still have some flexibility to access your cash. It's like having the best of both worlds—a bit more interest without sacrificing your ability to splurge on those must-have goodies.

Keep in mind, you may not want to put all your eggs in one basket. Spreading your savings across different options, often ensures greater financial security and is typically the smartest approach.

Watch Out for Money Traps

Ever heard of money drains? Yeah, they're out there. Lurking around like Dementors and silently eating away at your savings. Like casting a Patronus Charm to ward them off, here's how to safeguard your funds from these unseen dangers:

- **ATM Fees.** Picture this: you're out, need cash, and voila! You see a convenient ATM. But guess what? If it's not your bank's ATM, they likely will slap you with a fee. Solution? Plan your cash moves strategically. Find your bank's ATMs, or better yet, get your cashback from a grocery store. No fees, no drama.

- **Overdraft Fees.** This one's like a ninja—silent but deadly. Overdraft fees happen when you spend more than you have in your account. Sneaky, right? Keep tabs on your balance, set up alerts, and save yourself from the overdraft dilemma.

- **Monthly Maintenance Fees.** Some banks charge you a fee just for the "privilege" of holding your cash. Uh, no thanks. Look for no-fee or low-fee accounts. Your money deserves a safe spot but without the monthly rent.

- **Late Payment Fees.** Have you ever forgotten about a bill? Maybe not, since you're a teenager and probably don't have bills yet. Here's a harsh reality you have to look forward to. Missing a bill due date can be a money sinkhole. Set up reminders or automatic payments—whatever it takes to avoid those unnecessary late fees. Your money's got better places to be.

- **Subscription Sneak Attacks.** Subscription fees for things like streaming services, gym memberships or Xbox Game Pass can pile up and silently drain your funds. Review your subscriptions regularly, ditch what you don't need, and keep that cash where it belongs: in your pocket.

Avoiding money drains is like becoming a financial karate kid. It's all about staying vigilant, crafting a smart strategy, and skillfully deflecting unnecessary fees and expenses. This financial discipline ensures that every dollar you earn is not only saved but also works for you, building a stronger financial future.

Savings Account Comparison

Now, let's put the pen to the paper and find a savings account that's right for you! Check out Page 12 of your bonus workbook, where you'll find a savings account cheat sheet. Use this chart like your savings account navigator. Review it to ensure you understand the differences between the different account options you may encounter. When you're ready, start cruising for a savings account that will suit your needs and provide the most lucrative return on your hard-earned money. Once you've found three savings accounts that pique your interest, use Page 13 of your workbook to write down all the details and information you've researched. Use the comparison chart to help you determine which savings account would offer the service you want and deserve. And if you're feeling brave, take the leap and open an account!

Retirement?! But I'm Still in High School

Isn't retirement something only older people think about? Yes, that can be true. Older people do worry about retirement. But just because you're a newbie to the money game, doesn't mean it's too soon to think about retirement. I'm here to tell you that the sooner you get your retirement game on, the better your older years will be.

Be the Early Bird

Being the early bird isn't just about getting the worm; it's about snagging a supercharged retirement plan. Here's the scoop:

- **Time is Your BFF.** The earlier you start investing, the more time your cash has to grow. It's as simple as that. It's not just about the money you put in but about the time you give it to do its thing. Start early, and your money becomes a financial superhero with time as its sidekick.

- **Compound Interest Magic.** We've talked about this before, but it's worth repeating. Compound interest is like your money's superpower. Finding savings or investment options with better interest rates and returns, is a strategic move to consider making sooner, rather than later. Imagine it's like charging up your phone battery - the longer you leave it, the more power you get. Over time, a little bit of money can turn into a lot.

- **Less Stress, More Flex.** Starting early means you don't have to drop huge chunks of cash. You can start small and gradually amp it up. It's less stress on your wallet and more flexibility in your money moves. Even a small investment in your teenage years can snowball into a fat retirement down the road.

- **Riding the Market Waves.** We'll talk more about investing in Chapter 8, but it's worth giving a sneak peek here. Investing isn't about timing the market; it's about time in the market. Markets go up, markets go down, but over time, they generally go up. Starting early allows you to ride the waves, weather the storms, and come out on top.

Hopefully you see how starting early is the key to a comfortable retirement. It's like planting a tree today so you can enjoy the shade when you're older!

The Lowdown on Retirement Accounts

Continuing on the retirement topic, let's break down some typical retirement options you may have heard of or might encounter. If you're in the USA, the most common retirement plans you'll come across are a 401(k) and Roth IRAs. Let's go over the basics:

Traditional 401(k): The Workplace Rockstar

A 401(k) is a retirement account offered by your employer. It allows you to save money away *before* taxes. We'll discuss taxes more in

Chapter 9, but just know that anything Uncle Sam can't touch is a huge bonus. Plus, some companies drop in extra cash for you as an incentive to their employees. Free money alert!

Here's the deal: You can choose how much of your paycheck goes into the 401(k), so it's not just sitting there gathering dust. Sometimes you even get to play the investment maestro and pick where your money goes. The best part? It's like a money time machine. Your contributions grow, and you only pay taxes once you're living that retired life and cashing in.

Roth IRA: The Tax-Free Wizard

Now, say hello to Roth IRA, your magic ticket to tax-free savings in the retirement world. It's similar to a 401(k), but you fund it with your *after-tax* money. That means there's no immediate tax benefit, but, every penny you take out for your retirement is tax-free and yours to keep. So when you're enjoying your golden years and sipping a drink on the beach, Uncle Sam ain't knocking on your door. That's the Roth IRA promise – retirement bliss without a tax bill in sight.

Remember, both a traditional 401(k) and Roth IRA are like sidekicks in your journey to financial freedom. 401(k) gets you workplace perks and tax breaks today. A Roth IRA sets you up for a tax-free fiesta in retirement. Here's a helpful image you can refer back to, if you need a refresher on the differences:

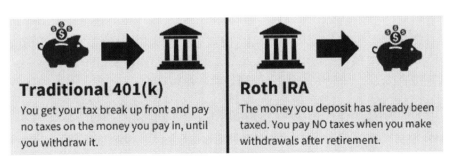

Traditional 401(k)
You get your tax break up front and pay no taxes on the money you pay in, until you withdraw it.

Roth IRA
The money you deposit has already been taxed. You pay NO taxes when you make withdrawals after retirement.

What If I'm Not in the USA?

Now, if you're not in the USA, don't worry! Other countries offer similar retirement options and benefits. For example, if you're in the UK you may have heard of a SIPP, a Self-Invested Personal Pension or your employer may offer a workplace pension. If you're in Canada, you may have heard of an RRSP, a Registered Retirement Savings Plan or a TFSA, a Tax-Free Savings Account. Both are excellent options and worth exploring. I've created a special page in your workbook outlining some common retirement plans for those teens not based out of the USA. Check out page 14 for further details.

Slow and Steady Wins The Race

Listen up because it's time to talk about the real MVP in the money game: consistency. It's not the flashy superstar, but trust me, it's the glue holding your financial empire together.

At first glance, small, consistent contributions might feel like spare change, but they have the potential to unlock the door to big financial wins down the road. It's like dropping pebbles in a pond—tiny ripples turn into bigger waves.

Imagine this: You're tossing a few bucks into your savings or investment account every week or month. Remember, it's not about the grand entrance; it's about showing up, rain or shine. Those regular contributions start building like a snowball rolling downhill, picking up speed and size. And that's where the magic happens. Your money isn't just sitting there; it's working 9 to 5, hustling, and making more money *for* you. Over time, those small, consistent contributions turn into a financial powerhouse.

Consistency is like Rocky preparing for a fight. Every day, you're doing those small reps and before you know it, you're knocking out the competitor! Don't believe me? Check out page 15 in your bonus workbook to see an example of a savings plan in action. Remember our 50/30/20 rule? 20% of your income should go towards savings.

Let's assume you're earning $200 a month through a part-time job or side hustle. You take what you've learned thus far and find a high-yield savings account that offers a 4% return and start putting $40 per month towards it. The chart illustrates how small but steady monthly contributions of $40, can balloon into $35,000 by the age of 50! And for a bit of inspiration, there's also a chart for $100 monthly contributions - because let's face it, you'll be earning more than $200 a month eventually, right? Maintaining the same growth rate and interest, you could build a staggering $87,000, by the age of 50! Never overlook the incredible impact of smart savings, the magic of compound interest, and the strength of consistency. These powerful forces combined, can unlock the doors to your financial freedom!

Next Up

Imagine Jenna, a teen financial whiz. Her summer job wasn't just for kicks; she was able to turn her paychecks into a financial force. And by the time Spring rolled around, she could finance her spring break adventure effortlessly, without dipping into her savings—a total victory!

Jenna understood that money has two roles: to be saved and to be enjoyed. But how do you make sure your spending game is on point? In the next chapter we talk about smart spending. We'll break down the art of spending, whether scoring the coolest gear or treating yourself to a fancy meal. And how to turn every dollar into a boss move. Meet you on the flip side!

6

Spend Wisely – Don't Get Played, Make the Play

M oney is a precious resource. But not for the reasons you might think. You see, money itself is only as valuable as the number of things you can buy with it.

Think about it.

Money is, ultimately, the way to get the things you need and want. That's why spending it wisely is crucial to mastering your money skills. Those who don't spend wisely tend to get played by the players. The "players" being those tricky folks who use hype to get you to drop your cash on the latest gadget, the trending TikTok product, and, well, you name it.

Mastering your spending means understanding the rules of the game. By understanding the strategies, you elevate your financial game to an all-star level. The ultimate aim? To take charge and call your own shots with confidence. This empowers you to control where your money flows, ensuring every move is meticulously planned.

So let's talk about how to become a money wizard from the start. Rather than letting your first paycheck vanish into a void, the goal is to resist the temptation to splurge on impulse buys or tricky scams.

My First Pay Day!

So, you've just snagged your first paycheck. Exciting! But now what? Let's break it down in a way that won't make your head spin faster than a rollercoaster.

Decoding Your Paycheck: Gross vs. Net

Alright, imagine your paycheck is a pizza. The entire pizza is your gross income. That's the total amount of your paycheck, before any deductions or taxes decide to crash the party.

Now, picture taking out slices for taxes, Social Security, health insurance, and maybe even a little piece for retirement. What's left after this slice-and-dice operation? That's your net income, the cold, hard cash you'll see in your bank account.

The Emotional Rollercoaster of Your First Paycheck

You know that feeling when you finally conquer that test you've been studying for all week? Multiply that by a hundred – that's the pride and excitement of getting your first paycheck. It's like adulting on expert mode and acing it.

But here's the catch: the temptation to spend that money can slowly sneak up on you. You might find yourself wanting to enjoy a fancy dinner, buy the latest gadget, or treat yourself to a day at the mall. After all, you deserve it, right? Those purchases may seem harmless at the moment, but it's the small leaks that sink big ships. Your first paycheck deserves respect, not a one-way ticket to spontaneous spending town.

Splurge Smarter, Not Harder

Let's dive into something super important: how to spend your money wisely. I'm not saying you should turn into a total Scrooge, hoarding every penny – that's no fun for anyone. But you also don't want to waste your cash on random things you'll forget about next week. The real deal is learning to spend smart. It's all about finding that sweet spot where you're enjoying your money but also making choices that make sense. Let's figure out how to use your cash in a way that's fun for you and good for your wallet.

Needs vs. Wants: The Psychology of Spending

Imagine needs and wants are like frenemies living in your brain. Needs are the essentials, like food, bills, and Wi-Fi. Wants, on the other hand, are the sparkly extras, like that shiny new gadget or style upgrade.

You've probably spotted something before and thought, "I absolutely NEED that," and convinced yourself to buy it without giving it much thought. But how often do you pause to consider if you truly need that shiny new object? Let's say you catch sight of the latest sneaker release, and your inner voice shouts, "I have to have them!" Unless your current pair is falling apart, chances are you don't *really* need them, right? It's likely more of a want than a need. And what happens when unexpected expenses, like an urgent car repair or a hefty phone bill, pop up? That's when the battle between needs and wants gets real. Knowing and recognizing the difference between what you want and what you need can make a huge difference in managing your finances effectively.

Something I do whenever I feel the urge to spend, is take a step back. Often, all I need to do is take a deep breath to gather my thoughts.

Then, ask myself is this item is something I *really* need? Most of the time, the answer is "no." So, I take my time deciding whether to splurge or not. Trust me. Limited-time offers are hardly "limited." Don't worry about missing out. That deal will come back around and you'll be in a better position to take advantage of it.

A Glimpse Into the Future: Bills and Expenses

Let's talk about a hypothetical scenario. You've spread your wings and left the nest. Congratulations! What comes along with getting your own place? Bills. They're like those unwelcomed guests who always show up uninvited. You're now responsible for rent, utilities, groceries, and maybe those sneaky subscription fees. These bills are eating away at your paycheck.

Here's the kicker: These bills won't RSVP; they waltz in whether you're ready or not. So, budgeting must become a vital part of your routine. It helps you tackle these unexpected expenses without breaking a sweat. Remember to prioritize your bills. Essentials like heat, water, and electricity are necessary to live comfortably. Another thing to keep an eye out for are those credit card payments. Don't let them get buried in the mix of your other bills. Building these habits will pay off as you move on to bigger and better things like car payments and mortgages.

Sale Alert: Is It Really a Steal?

Sale signs, discounts, and the ever-enticing "limited-time offer." Ah, the siren songs of the shopping world. Here's a secret – just because it's on sale doesn't mean it's a steal. Companies are like sly magicians, using psychology to make you think you're getting a bargain.

Take Amazon Prime Day, for example. It's a shopping fiesta, but not every deal is your golden ticket. Prices can be inflated before the sale, making that 'discount' less thrilling in reality. So, before you click 'buy now,' do a little price history check. You might be surprised to find that sales aren't really sales. If you play your cards right, you can find great deals throughout the entire year!

Impulse Buying: The Sneaky Bandit Strikes Again

An impulse buy is that urge to buy something without a second thought, fueled by the adrenaline of your hard-earned money. We've all been there. The flashy sale signs or the "limited-time" offer that's as tempting as a chocolate fountain at a dessert table. Impulse buying is the trickster of the spending world. It's like a ninja sneaking up on you when you least expect it. So what's your secret weapon? Patience. Instead of diving headfirst into the 'Buy Now' frenzy, try taking a step back.

Recognizing impulse buying is like putting on superhero glasses. Once you see it for what it is, you can dodge the bullets. Why? Because while these purchases may seem unassuming at first, they can add up quickly. You might find yourself blowing your entire paycheck without even realizing it!

Remember to reflect on whether you're splurging smarter or just falling into the impulse-buying trap. Your finances will thank you. Plus, splurging smarter means you can swap out things for experiences. Consider memories over material! Because let's face it, that concert spent with mates or an epic weekend getaway is way cooler than another gadget collecting dust.

Keep in mind that we all make mistakes now and again. Sometimes you can't help yourself. You fall into the temptation of a limited-time sale or special offer. Don't worry. It happens to all of us. The key is to keep your eyes on the prize. Don't sweat it if it happens once. Just make sure it doesn't become a habit.

The Impulse Buying Challenge

Ever heard of the Impulse Purchase Delay Technique? It's like a Jedi mind trick for your wallet. Here's how it works:

A Week to Resist Temptation

Picture this: You're strolling through the mall, and there it is – the shiny, tempting swag you never knew you needed. Your gut says, "Buy it now!" But hold up. Instead of diving headfirst into the impulse-buying abyss, let's try the Impulse Purchase Delay Technique.

Challenge yourself to stop, and make a pact with the future you. Say, "Alright, cool item, I see you. But let's wait a week before making this official." It's like a commitment ceremony for your wallet.

The One-Week Waiting Game: Do You Still Want It?

Now, here's where the magic happens. Let that item marinate in your thoughts for a week. Why? Because emotions can be tricky. The initial excitement could wear off, and may help you recognize if it's a fling or the real deal.

Ask yourself some questions during this waiting period:

- **Do I *Really* Need It?** The age-old question. Can your life go on without this item, or is it actually necessary?

- **Why Do I Want It?** Dig deep. Is it a genuine need, or are you just caught up in the moment? Sometimes, the desire fades once the initial buzz wears off.

- **Can I Afford It Without Stress?** Money talks, and so does financial peace. If buying this won't send your budget into a tailspin, great. If it does though, perhaps you should reconsider.

The Power of Reflection: Why Do You Still Want It?

After the week-long waiting game, if you still find yourself drooling over that item, congrats! You've just pulled off a mindful purchase. Now, ask yourself why. What makes it worth the investment? Is it a quality item, a genuine need, or does it bring you lasting joy?

Maybe it's that ergonomic chair your back's been dreaming of, or perhaps it's a gadget that sparks a smile every time you use it. Knowing the why behind the want helps you make smarter decisions and keeps your spending in check.

Don't forget, it's not about denying yourself the enjoyment of fun purchases. It's about making smarter choices. Reflecting on your purchases is the best way to stop the gravitational pull of impulse buying. Letting things sit for a week may be the trick to keep your cash from flying away!

Impulse Journal Exercise

As homework for this chapter, I want you to keep track of 3 items, or "shiny objects" as I like to call them, which caught your attention. These shiny objects tend to create an impulse or a sense of urgency to make a purchase.

The idea is to execute the impulse purchase delay technique, and document your answers to the questions you should be asking yourself. This allows you to better reflect on your spending choices. For example, if something catches your eye online or in a store, and you feel an impulse to buy that item, pause and use the impulse journal (on Page 17 of your workbook) to write down some of your immediate thoughts. Why did that item catch your eye? Why did you feel like you wanted it? Do you really need it? Can you afford it? Then, practice the waiting game. Give it a few days to see if you still feel like you want or need that item. Or, if the impulse has passed. The more you practice this approach, the more mindful you will become of your spending.

Guarding Your Fortress & Avoiding Scams

It's time to talk about keeping your money safe. Imagine you are the guardian of your money galaxy, protecting your cash from anyone trying to infiltrate. Believe it or not, there are people out there who want a piece of your hard-earned cash and will go to great lengths to swipe it from you. But don't worry. I'm here to help! Let's focus on keeping your money safe and sound, ensuring you're the only one calling the shots on how it's used and where it's spent.

Spotting Scams: Because "Too Good to Be True" Usually Is

First things first, if it seems too good to be true, it probably is. That Nigerian prince offering you a fortune? Yeah, that's the classic "too good to be true" scam. So, embrace your inner skeptic. Look out for sketchy emails, shady websites, and messages that reek of desperation. Scammers are sneaky, but you can be ready for them!

Protecting Your Personal Info

Your personal info is like the golden ticket to Scam City. So, lock it up tighter than Fort Knox. Use passwords that are tougher to crack than a secret agent code. Mix in numbers and symbols to keep it more challenging to hack. And for that extra layer of protection, turn on two-factor authentication when the option is available. It's like having a beefed-up bouncer at the VIP entrance to your accounts.

Best Practices 101: A Crash Course in Scam-Proof Living

Here are some tips to avoid getting scammed:

- **Loose Lips Sink Ships.** Remember not to spill your info to anyone who asks. Your personal details are like your phone's passcode – only share with those you trust.

- **Password Protection.** Make your passwords as unique as your fingerprint. And change them regularly to maintain security.

- **Phishy Business.** Phishing is a common practice where scammers send emails or messages, pretending to be someone they're not, to trick you into revealing personal information. Spot phishing emails by checking for dodgy URLs and weird grammar. If it smells fishy, it's probably a phishing attempt.

- **Social Media Street Smarts.** Watch out for social media scams – they're the pickpockets of the digital world. Don't accept candy (or friend requests) from strangers.

- **Easy Money Illusions.** If someone promises easy money, it's probably a magic trick – and not the good kind. Avoid falling for the temptation of quick cash schemes.

- **Stranger Danger (Online Edition).** Are you getting cold callers and random messages from strangers? There's an easy solution. Delete. Block. Repeat.

- **Evaluate Those 5-Star Reviews.** Channel your inner Sherlock Holmes when reading online reviews. If they appear too good to be true, they probably are. Scammers are masters at orchestrating fake and glowing reviews.

What to Do If You've Been Hit

If you think you've stumbled into a scam, no need to freak out. I know it might be downright terrifying to realize you've been scammed. But the worst thing you can do is panic. When sneaky folks scam you, there are things you can do to prevent something like that from happening again:

- Call your local police to report the scammers' number. The police can give you more information about filing a report.

- Call or visit your bank to review charges or withdrawals.

- Take note of names, emails, phone numbers, and social media profiles of people you interacted with.

- Take screenshots of text messages.

- Contact your phone company to see if recordings of calls between you and the fraudster are available.

- Ask your phone company for records to investigate numbers you received calls or messages from.

Another good rule of the thumb is to report the scam to trusted agencies. This can help stop the bad guys and keep others safe. Here's a list of safe places to report scams:

FTC (Federal Trade Commission) – Your go-to squad for nailing scam artists

- Website: https://www.ftc.gov/

- Report a scam here: https://reportfraud.ftc.gov/#/

- Phone Number: 1-877-FTC-HELP (1-877-382-4357)

Better Business Bureau (BBB) – Allows you to view and report scams in your area

- Website: https://www.bbb.org/scamtracker

FBI's Internet Crime Complaint Center (IC3) – Dedicated to receiving complaints about internet-related crimes

- Website: https://www.ic3.gov/ (and click on "File a Complaint")

Anti-Phishing Working Group (APWG) – Report phishing emails and websites

- Website: https://apwg.org/

- Email: reportphishing@apwg.org

Regularly reviewing your passwords, email accounts, and social media profiles is also a good practice. A good security checkup can help prevent further attacks. It might be a drag, but it's totally worth keeping your personal information safe.

Common Scams to Look Out For

I've created a handy reference guide for you with some of the most common scams and red flags to be on the lookout for. Check out Page 16 of your bonus workbook. If ever necessary, reference this guide to pause and check if you might be falling victim to a scam.

Next Up

This chapter has certainly been a wild ride. Fighting the urge to spend your cash can be trickier than wrestling a crocodile. But hopefully, you can now see why mastering the habit of controlling impulse buying can lead the way to becoming a money guru.

The best part is, your consistent and mindful efforts will help you build effective money-management habits. Soon enough, you won't have to think twice about what to do. You'll be well-prepared to respond, especially when facing the sparkling lights of special offers and limited-time sales.

So what's next? We're tackling credit. Imagine credit like your social media profile. You want your posts and stories to reflect the best version of yourself, right? Well, managing credit is similar. You want it to reflect the best version of your financial persona. A well-managed credit score is like a profile with a strong following and positive engagement—it opens doors to exclusive opportunities, from loans to jobs. Neglect it, and it's like letting your social media slip into a mess, where recovery takes time. We'll dive into how to maintain a stellar financial profile, ensuring you're always swipe-right worthy in the eyes of lenders. Ready to get those likes up?

7

Credit, Debt, and Scores – Keep Yours on Point

Don't you love it when you get hit by tons of likes and DMs after posting your latest pics? Yeah, we all love the feeling of knowing you're rocking the best looks. But you know what else is cool? Rocking your credit game. Sure, you might not get tons of likes on Insta by posting your credit score. But having top-notch credit is something you can't afford to pass up. As you start to master your credit you unlock so many bonus levels and hidden treasures.

Don't believe me?

Let's talk about why acing your credit score is totally worth it. You'll not only gain access to the tools you need to succeed, but you'll also avoid the sneaky pitfalls that come along with debt.

Credit and Debt 101

You may have heard about credit and debt. Or how they often get a bad rap. Usually, though, that comes from people who've gotten in trouble with them. But if you talk to folks who really understand credit and debt, they'll dish out the good stuff and spill it positively. Seriously. The folks that know how the credit game is played, won't dis it. They'll tell you how awesome it is to have credit on your side. Good credit and mindful use of debt is like getting extra lives in a game. Let's start with the basics.

The Basics of Credit

- **Credit types**. Credit comes in various shapes and sizes. We've got installment credit, which includes loans for big-ticket items like cars and houses. You borrow a lump sum of money and pay it back in fixed amounts over time. Then there's revolving credit, which is more for credit cards. With revolving credit, you have a credit limit, and as long as you make at least the minimum payments, you can keep using it.

- **Credit score**. Your credit score is like your financial report card. It's a number that ranges from 300 to 850, and it tells the people who might be loaning you money how trustworthy you are. Things like paying bills on time, having and managing different types of credit, and keeping credit card balances low, can boost your score.

So, why does this all matter?

Good credit can be your financial passport. It's not just about getting a credit card or a loan; it could affect your ability to rent an apartment, buy a car, or even land a job. Think of credit like those bonus points in your favorite video game. When you're dreaming of big buys like your first car or even a house, having good credit is like unlocking those extra levels that make reaching your goals easier. Sure, you could try to get there without credit, but it's like playing a game on hard mode without any cheats or boosts.

All About Debt

Debt. Sounds like a bad thing, right? It doesn't have to be, if you play it smartly. Savvy financial wizards know that debt can actually be a good thing when used correctly. When misused, however, it can quickly ruin your life faster than having a concert canceled on you. Let's talk about how debt can either make a great impact, or create a terrible experience.

- **Good debt vs. bad debt.** Good debt is an investment in your future. Student loans, for example, can lead to a better-paying job. Mortgages help you build equity in a home. Bad debt, on the other hand, is money spent on things that don't offer the potential to grow in value (or "appreciate," as some say), like that pricey weekend getaway or the latest tech gadget.

- **Challenges in paying off debt.** Paying off debt can feel like a marathon. Unexpected expenses pop up, making allocating extra money towards debt tough. There's also a psychology aspect behind it – instant gratification vs. delayed reward. It takes discipline and sometimes sacrifice to chip away at debt.

A good way to look at debt is to only bite off what you can chew. Always consider and calculate how you can pay off the debt, before jumping into it. Those small monthly re-payments can pile up fast, turning into a huge snowball that could knock you flat. Carefully considering debt before you dive in, can prevent you from drowning in it.

Unfortunately, if you end up in debt trouble, you may realize that being sent to the principal's office was actually a walk in the park by comparison.

The Benefit of Credit Cards

Credit cards can be your financial sidekick, offering a dynamic duo of convenience and opportunity. Let's look at some of the key benefits they bring to the table.

- **Credit card rewards.** There's no such thing as free money, right? Wrong! Many credit cards offer rewards like cash back, travel points, or discounts on purchases. Some cards even have sign-up bonuses that feel like uncovering a secret jackpot. The key is to find a card that aligns with your spending habits and lifestyle.

- **Using credit cards wisely.** To truly benefit from credit cards, you've got to be on your A-game. Pay the full balance each month to avoid those nasty interest charges. Set up automatic payments and monitor your statements closely for any funny business.

- **Building credit with credit cards**. Credit cards are not just about spending; they're a tool for building credit. Responsible use—making on-time payments and keeping balances low—can boost your credit score. It's like a financial win-win. You see, credit card companies report your behavior to the credit bureaus that determine your credit score. This situation is like your teachers telling your parents how you've behaved at school. If you behave well, you get rewarded. If you don't, you get the financial equivalent of detention. And believe me, financial detention is not a fun thing.

As you can see, finances and money become much easier with credit. The key is to know how to play your cards right, literally.

Now, let's get into your credit score and why you need to pay close attention to it.

Yes, Your Credit Score Matters

How important is your GPA and SAT score, when submitting those college applications? Pretty crucial, right? Ask anyone with bad grades how hard it can be to get into the college of their choice.

The same goes for your credit score. Unfortunately, doors tend to get slammed in your face if you have poor credit. However, you'll likely get the red carpet treatment if you have a great credit score. Let's find out why.

How Is Your Credit Score Calculated?

Credit scores are numerical representations of your creditworthiness, and they play a crucial role in determining your ability to borrow money and the rates you might receive. Here's how they're calculated:

- **Payment History:** Your track record of paying bills on time is the most significant factor, determining for 35% of your credit score. Late or missed payments, can significantly lower your score.

- **Credit Utilization:** The utilization of your credit, determines 30% of your score. It measures how much of your available credit you're using. Keeping your utilization low, ideally below 35% of your total credit limit, signals that you're managing your credit well.

- **Length of Credit History:** This is essentially a record of how long you've been handling your money. Longer credit histories are viewed more favorably because they provide more data on your borrowing behavior. This includes the age of your oldest and newest account, as well as the average age of all your other accounts. Credit history determines 10% of your credit score.

- **Types of Credit in Use:** Having different types of credit accounts, determines 10% of your credit score. If you have a good mix of accounts it can have a positive impact, as it demonstrates that you're capable of managing different types of credit effectively.

- **New Credit:** Opening several new credit accounts in a short period can be seen as risky behavior and may lower your score. Keep in mind, this includes the number of recent inquiries from any credit accounts which you've applied for. New credit activity rounds out our calculation and determines that final 10% of your credit score.

Understanding these factors can help you take steps to improve or maintain a good credit score.

What's a Good Credit Score?

All right, so we know how a credit score is calculated. But what does a good credit score actually look like?

Think of it like a school grade. A good credit score is basically the A+ of the financial report card. We're talking about a number strutting around like it owns the place, that lenders give high-fives to.

If you're rocking a score of 700 or above, you're in the honors club. That's like having a backstage pass to the concert of life. You get the best deals on loans, credit cards practically throw themselves at you, and landlords are begging you to rent their primo apartments.

Now, if you're in the 600s, it's not a disaster zone, but it's like getting a B or a solid B-. You're not wearing the crown but still a respectable ruler of your financial kingdom. Lenders might not throw roses at your feet, but they won't slam the door in your face, either.

Dropping under 600, though, is like getting a C or below. It's not exactly detention-worthy, but you might find yourself in the not-so-exclusive club of higher interest rates and lenders hesitant to work with you. They're giving you the side-eye, wondering if you're the responsible borrower they're looking for.

Keep in mind if your credit score does start to dip, there are steps you can take to turn things around. By making a few strategic moves, you can help get your score back on track and position yourself to enjoy the perks of a solid credit rating.

Factors That Impact Your Credit Score

As you can probably guess, the factors used to calculate your credit score, also have a huge impact on it. Let's review more closely why on-time payments, credit utilization, and credit history play big role in your credit score journey.

On-time payments are like the anchor of your credit score. They signal to credit bureaus that you're dependable and serious about your financial commitments. Consistently paying on time can significantly elevate your score. However, missing a payment is similar to that of a weak link in a chain and will likely result in damage to your credit health. Late payments can also rapidly deteriorate your score, kind of like rust can weaken metal.

Credit utilization is the balancing act of your financial portfolio. Think of it as a professional juggler tossing multiple beanbags in the air. Your credit cards are these beanbags; you want to use them skillfully without dropping them. Maintaining a low balance is like a juggler flawlessly executing his routine, which impresses the audience (or the credit bureaus in this case) and boosts your score. Maxing out your cards, however, is like a juggling mishap that can send your score plummeting.

Lastly, credit history is the seasoned navigator of your credit journey. It's like having a skilled captain at the helm of a ship, guiding you through the financial seas. The longer you've been managing your credit effectively, the more trust you build, enhancing your credit score. It's not just about how many accounts you have but how well you've managed them over time. If you're new to credit, think of yourself as an apprentice navigator still learning the ropes. With time and consistent good habits, you'll become a pro at steering your credit score into more favorable waters.

How to Get Started

So, you're standing at the starting line of the credit marathon, scratching your head and wondering, "Where the heck do I even begin?" Fear not, because we're about to map out a strategy for you to turn that credit scoreboard from zero to hero.

Getting Off the Starting Line

- **Find a Secured or Starter Credit Card.** A secured credit card is one that requires a cash security deposit when you open the account. The deposit is held as collateral in case you fail to make the monthly payments. On the other hand, a starter credit card is designed for folks with no or limited credit history and usually offers a lower credit limit. Both options require you to be 18 years old, if you don't have a co-signer.

- **Leverage Family Support.** If you're not 18 years old yet or getting your own card seems too daunting, consider having a parent co-sign on a credit card or becoming an authorized user on one of their cards. This arrangement allows you to benefit from their established credit history, giving your credit score a boost as you demonstrate responsible use. Just remember, this requires mutual trust and clear communication about spending habits and limits.

- **Embrace the Power of Tiny Purchases.** Start small, my friend. It's not about buying a yacht; it's about dipping your toes in the credit pool. Grab a coffee, maybe a sandwich – keep it simple. This demonstrates to credit authorities that you can manage your finances effectively without jeopardizing your budget.

- **The Essential Practice of Timely Payments**: On-time payments are your financial ace in the hole. Treat them as a non-negotiable monthly routine, similar to any other ritual you can't live without. It's more than just dodging late fees; it's about proving to credit bureaus you're a committed and reliable borrower.

Now that you're off to the races, let's consider the crucial dos and don'ts of credit:

Dos:

- **Stay Cool with Your Credit Limits**: Don't max out your credit cards. It's like knowing how to groove at a party – you want to have fun but not go overboard. Keeping your credit use low is like being smooth and savvy with your spending.

- **Set Up Auto-Pay**: Consider automatic payments, like setting reminders for your favorite TV shows. It ensures you never miss a payment, keeping your credit score healthy and happy.

- **Grow Your Credit History**: The longer you use credit responsibly, the better. It's like adding cool stories to your social media over time. Each one makes your overall profile more interesting and shows you're reliable and consistent.

Don'ts

- **Steer Clear of Maxing Out**: Hitting your credit card's limit isn't a goal to shoot for. Maxing out your card is like trying to dance on ice – it can quickly lead to a slippery mess.

- **Don't Neglect Your Bills**: Forgetting or ignoring your bills is a common mistake. Failing to make payments can drastically impact your credit score, an outcome you'll want to steer clear of.

- **Avoid a Credit Card Frenzy**: Opening or applying for too many credit cards isn't a winning strategy. This could lead to overspending and make it harder to manage your accounts effectively. Concentrate on finding one or two main cards that you can handle responsibly to build your credit score with. Remember quality over quantity.

Hopefully, it's clear by now that responsibility is the name of the game. Maxing out credit can be fun for a while. But soon enough, debt will catch up to you. When it does, you'll be in a world of hurt. So, start slow and take it easy. You can always add to your debt as you gain more experience and find sensible ways of using debt to your advantage.

The Dark Side of Debt

Unfortunately, and as you may have already guessed, debt has a dark side. And it's darker than becoming a Sith lord. It can trash your creditworthiness, leaving you in a tough spot. Ask anyone who's ever been there. It takes years to recover from. And during this time, you'll be unable to access any of the perks of good credit history. Let's take a deeper look.

The Debt Snowball

Debt is like a snowball. It starts small and then grows as it rolls down the hill. Eventually, crushing you and taking you down with it. Here's why:

- **Small Debts, Big Impact**: Think of your debts as tiny

snowflakes. They may seem harmless initially, but as they accumulate, they form a massive snowball. Even small debts can spiral into a financial crisis if not managed properly.

- **The Minimum Payment Dilemma**: Sure, it may be tempting to only pay what you need to on your credit cards. But paying just the minimum is like trying to stop a snowball with a small shovel. It barely makes an impact and merely delays the inevitable. Plus, that sneaky interest rate acts as fuel, causing the debt to grow rapidly, much like a snowball gaining momentum downhill.

- **Speaking of Interest**: In Chapter 5, we explored how compound interest can benefit your savings by growing your money. However, when it comes to debt, compound interest works against you. The longer your debt stays unpaid, the more it compounds, creating a more significant financial burden over time. It's essential to recognize and tackle it when necessary – or it'll tackle you.

Crisis Control Tips

The key to effective debt management is knowing how to handle a crisis. Here are some tips:

- **Solid Budgeting**: Establish a strong budget to protect your finances. Monitor your spending, cut back on non-essentials, and guard against impulsive purchases. Think of it as creating a secure boundary for your financial well-being.

- **Emergency Funds as a Safety Net**: Setting up an emergency fund is like having a safety net for unexpected financial situations. Life can be unpredictable, but with a reserve fund, you're prepared for those sudden expenses.

- **Navigating Financial Hazards**: Learn from others' debt experiences. Steer clear of payday loans, high-interest credit cards, and unnecessary debts. It's about making smart choices and avoiding common financial traps.

- **Confronting Major Debt**: You likely won't have any significant debt in the near future. However, if you do find yourself racking up substantial debt, it's best to address it head-on. Focus on debts with high interest rates first and allocate extra funds to them. It's like strategically tackling your biggest financial challenge.

In essence, managing your debt effectively is about applying smart strategies to maintain control over your finances. So be sure to equip yourself with these skills to avoid the dark side of debt.

The Credit Score Checklist

Building your credit score is a journey. I've created a handy credit score checklist that you can reference and use. It contains helpful best practices and action items you can take to build and improve your credit score over time. Be sure to check out Page 18 of your bonus workbook!

Next Up

As we close the chapter on credit and debt, hopefully, you feel better equipped to navigate this area more confidently. Next, we venture into the realm of investing. The upcoming chapter simplifies the basics of investing, from understanding key terms to diversifying your portfolio. You'll discover how teenagers like you have achieved investment success and learn the crucial balance between risk and reward.

Investing is a vital step towards financial independence, allowing your money to grow even as you sleep. Ready to unlock the secrets of making your savings work for you? Let's dive into the world of investing, where smart choices today can lead to a prosperous tomorrow.

Before we get into the next chapter, let's take a break to try a word search. As you hunt down these words, reflect on the significance of each one. Has your understanding or insight changed on any of them since starting this book?

```
Q X S E U M X F P B Z J S C A R I K Z D X X N K M J G V X H
F T K O L K O D Y H S L I Z Y P N Z B U G O T X N B G H Q D
E A M T D W C N X Z M Y E W H F Z T K Z R B X U Q K N Z F I
E X P E N S E P E H G Q R O E P Q V W T V C W L O Q T M L Q
V M H Q B S U C Y Y N N L X X H N Q X F O I K N B I S F D B
B J Q R E F S C S I K Y E S C O F D D C R E D I T C A R D T
R U L H W B U M A L M J V U H Z N T K Y O K M S X R K A Z C
I E D X J H P Q V Y V H B M X B I L L S E H S I F X A T Z A
L I T G P P Q V I A C R H D V K K B K C Q G H S R T B N E Q
A S G I E Z I F N I R B A N K S Z H T C C D I P U E D J L L
W V V W O R T E O G H Z L O I N B Y E Q R K T P E Y O N A J X
Y J X Q P E E D K P J R J M D Q W R Q E P O M N X L S U C O
T H V L T I M J H Y I L T P X N K P P D F H Q D S H L I X L
T J P O S S O E K E W Z D U J T T M J I M Q T I Z H V D Q S
X D J Y M N L L N C K G T L T S J L X T G H L N H X B Q F W
H C S H N E I M R T L Y P S D D O R G D A K Q G U Z D M D T
D N K B L V N Q K Y B K N E C F G X N L P C T K A Z A T N V
R Y E P N K T F Y F G U U U X I L L L P O A W I A G C W A F
A L P D D Z E Q B K O V E N T E D N S B Y S B X D L C I E S
T S P K I Y R Z B Y N R V X P N O R E J C H Z K U I O M E S
V P E V A T E X P M K G T R F Q P A Y C H E C K F H U X I C
T F R N N X S G I A Z T H S G H N G E F N S Y A R H N F C A
M X P X P F T E A H Y C G W S B T Z D I O F J B F K T D H M
O L H C P R W G R N T M W J Q Q L Y W O Z G P J C X M L K S
I P H W L C S I S R C B E L F B N F J O Z C D E Q G O G K E
F D L O P H H H P H A G V N Y Q Z X R T B H W E G S X S L H
F D S E T L U L B R V T X K T B X J A T P O Z Q B M C H B L
Y X S H E W F P K L K F E S B M W O D H M O U R A T D O B P
J P M I B V C H F S E P H O D B E D M R D F A R O N G M R W
B N S Q F E R X Q X C V Y L D T D U D J M K M Z O P Q J N E
```

DEBT	RATE	SPENDING	PAYCHECK
PAYMENT	BUDGET	BILLS	MONEY
IMPULSE	SAVING	CREDIT	RETIREMENT
SCAMS	SCORE	BANK	CASH
CREDITCARD	EXPENSE	ACCOUNT	INTEREST

8

Investing – Earn Right, While You Sleep Tight

How often have you imagined living your dream life, complete with a luxury car, a beautiful home, the latest gadgets, and surrounded by loved ones? Turning dreams into a reality may not be as farfetched as you think. It all boils down to knowing how to earn money right, even while you sleep.

Don't believe me?

Try Googling Erik Finman. He went from investing $1,000 at the age of 12 to turning it into millions by the age of 18. It just takes a little know-how and a lot of action to go from zero to hero in the investment game. In this chapter we focus on how you can become your own version of Erik Finman. So, hang tight because a ton of helpful information is headed your way!

Start Small, Dream Big

The key to investing is to start somewhere. There is never a "perfect" time to start investing. You just have to take the first step. From there, you can begin building your empire, or your "portfolio," as some might call it. You can start small or start big. It doesn't really matter. As long as you start somewhere.

The Basics of Investing

Unlike savings, where your money sits in a safe place earning a fixed interest, investing involves putting your money into assets with the expectation of generating a profit. It's a bit like planting seeds; you put in a little, nurture it over time, and watch it grow into something more significant.

Investing is a great way to make your money grow over time. Let me explain how it works:

When you invest with outside sources, like banks or stock markets, your money becomes available to others. It can then serve a variety of purposes, such as providing mortgages or financing for businesses. In return, you get paid. Think of this payment as a reward for allowing someone else to use your money instead of using it for yourself.

You can also invest in your own business. Doing so allows your money to work for *you* and not others. You invest money up-front, with the ultimate goal of turning it into more money. Think of a small business idea, something like selling t-shirts online. You need money to get your business going, right? Buy shirts, hire a designer, build a website, etc. Once you start selling your shirts, the goal is to make back that initial investment. Then, once you break even, you have an opportunity to multiply your money as you make more sales.

Now, let's consider a detailed example, focused on investing in stocks:

Imagine you have $500 that you want to invest. You've been keeping an eye on the tech industry, and you're particularly interested in a company called NexGen Tech. You've done some research, read some news articles, and feel confident that NexGen Tech is poised for growth.

Now, here's where the investment magic happens. You decide to buy shares of NexGen Tech. Each share is currently priced at $50. With your $500, you can purchase 10 shares ($500 / 50 shares = 10).

Fast forward a few months, and your research pays off – NexGen Tech releases a groundbreaking product, and its stock value increases. The new share price now stands at $70. If you decide to sell your 10 shares at this new price, you'll make a profit. Let's do the math: 10 shares multiplied by $70 = $700. Subtract your initial investment of $500, and you're left with with a $200 profit.

To review this detailed example:

- Original Investment Amount: $500
- Company: NexGen Tech
- Initial Share Price: $50
- Number of Shares Purchased: 10
- New Share Price: $70
- Profit: $200

This example illustrates the basic concept of buying low and selling high – a fundamental principle in investing. Of course, in the real world, factors like market conditions, company performance, and unforeseen events play a role, but the essence remains the same.

Asset Portfolio

Picture your investments like a sports team – each player has a unique role, and together, they can create a winning combination. In the investing world, this lineup of different players is known as your "asset portfolio." Spreading your investments across various assets, like stocks, bonds or real estate, helps balance your risk. It increases the likelihood of growing your money over time. Think of it as not putting all your eggs in one basket – a wise move in the financial kitchen!

Understanding your asset portfolio is crucial because it reflects your financial goals, risk tolerance, and ideal time lines. Some assets may offer higher returns but come with greater risk, while others are more stable but offer lower returns. Finding the right balance is key.

Boosting Your Financial Game

Now, here's the exciting part. Young investors like yourself can significantly boost their financial game with dedication, a solid strategy, and a sprinkle of luck. Think of it as being in a marathon where your money gradually increases in value the longer you stay in the race. Remember though, investing does involve risk, so it's crucial to educate yourself and be aware of potential pitfalls.

Investing as a Teen

The thought of investing as a teenager might sound daunting. Fortunately, there are fantastic platforms and apps designed specifically for young investors. Enter the world of micro-investing, where you can start with pocket change. If you're in the USA, apps like Acorns or Robinhood allow you to invest small amounts, making it accessible and less intimidating. If you're in the UK, you may want to check out the EToro app. And if you're in Canada be sure to take a look at the Moka app. These apps allow you to dip your toes into the investment pool before taking a full plunge.

Consider setting aside a portion of your earnings or allowances for investing. This not only helps you get into the habit, but also encourages financial discipline early on. Remember, it's not about the amount you start with but the consistency of your contributions.

Diversifying Your Portfolio

Think of diversification as mixing things up, rather than sticking to the same routine every day. You probably like to keep it fresh and mix up your style, right? That's how you should approach your investing. Smart investors distribute their assets amongst multiple options to ensure greater safety and balance. This helps significantly reduce risk. Let's discuss what these different options may look like:

Diversification: Your Portfolio's Superpower

As mentioned earlier, your portfolio is like a sports team, with each player bringing a unique set of skills to the table. Each type of investment offers strengths and weaknesses. Diversification involves spreading your investments across different types of assets. Why is this crucial? Well, if one area takes a hit (during tough times in the market for example), the others can help balance the losses. It's like having a Swiss army knife to help weather the storm.

Some Common Investment Options

Let's start with some basic terms you might hear in the investment world:

- **First up are Stocks**. When you buy a stock, you essentially own a tiny piece of a company. If the company does well, so do you; if not, your investment might decrease.

- **Next, we have Bonds.** Imagine lending money to a company or the government, and in return, they pay you back with a little extra. Bonds are usually less risky than stocks and offer a more predictable stream of income.

- **Then, there are Mutual Funds**. Picture a group project where everyone combines their money into one big "mutual" pot. A professional then uses this pool of money to invest in a variety of stocks and bonds.

- **Finally, we have Exchange-Traded Funds (or ETFs)**. ETFs are a lot like mutual funds but are bought and sold just like stocks.

To get more comfortable, consider user-friendly platforms which allow you to buy and sell these investments with ease. If you're in the USA Robinhood or E*TRADE are great options. If you're in the UK, Freetrade or Hargreaves Lansdown may be helpful. And If you're in Canada Questrade or CIBC can be great starting platforms.

Bitcoin and Beyond

I'm sure you've heard of Bitcoin or cryptocurrencies. Think of them as the trendsetters in the digital world. Bitcoin is like the digital version of gold, a currency that isn't controlled by any central authority. On the other hand, Ethereum is more than just money – it's a platform where people can build their own crypto apps and coins. If you're curious, platforms like Coinbase or Binance (offered only in the USA) offer a gateway into the crypto investing world. Remember though, the crypto market can be wild, so start small and educate yourself further before diving in.

Future Investment Opportunities

Let's look beyond the usual stocks and crypto to see what other cool investment opportunities might be on the horizon.

Real estate remains a classic investment option. Owning property is more than just finding a home; it's an investment that typically grows in value over time. Whether you're buying a place for yourself or finding a house or apartment to rent out, property ownership is a solid way to earn some extra cash on the side.

Airbnb rentals have emerged as a modern twist on traditional property renting. With the rise of the sharing economy, owning a property that can be rented out short-term on platforms like Airbnb lets you take advantage of tourists or big events in town. As a bonus, you often make more money than you typically would from normal renting.

What about investing in the planet's future? Green tech and renewable energy, like solar panels or wind farms, are not just good for the Earth – they could be good for your wallet too. As the world gets greener, these eco-friendly investments might start paying off big time.

Diving into different investments is like loading your financial toolkit with all sorts of cool gadgets. Whether you're into the classic vibe of owning stocks and bonds, getting into the new wave of crypto, or making money off a place to stay, there's a whole world for you to explore. Just remember, the trick to winning the money game is mixing things up and keeping an eye on what's next. Your money's journey is just beginning, so gear up, stay curious, and build that dream portfolio one smart move at a time.

Turn Your Passion into Profit

You may have heard about people who've turned their personal passions into profitable projects. Sounds like a dream come true, right? It doesn't have to be just a dream, though. You really can hit a home run with your passion projects if you have the know-how to start turning a hobby into a side gig. And hey, who knows? You may be able to transform that side gig into a real money-making machine. Let's dig deeper:

Investing Time in Personal Projects

Turning your passion into profit is not just a catchy phrase; it's actually something that's achievable. Take starting a YouTube channel, for instance. Imagine you love gaming – by sharing your gameplay, providing reviews, or creating entertaining content, you're not only engaging with a community but also opening doors to potential revenue through ad partnerships and sponsorships. Similarly, you can tap into your unique skills and transform them into marketable products. For example, developing an app or selling custom artwork. It's an investment not just in your time but in the potential growth of something you genuinely love.

Brands and Passions Are More than Just Fandom

Your love for certain brands or hobbies can be a gateway to financial education and growth. Start by researching the companies behind your favorite products. Understand their financial reports, how well they're positioned in the market, and their growth strategies. Once you've grasped the business side, consider investing in their stocks. For example, if you're a tech enthusiast, dive into the world of tech giants like Apple or Google. Your knowledge on their products can give you better insights into their potential success.

Real-Life Teenage Investment Wins

So, how realistic is it to become a millionaire in your teens? Well, not too common, but it turns out that striking gold as a teen is achievable. Here are some stories to spark some inspiration:

- **Erik Finman.** His early investment in Bitcoin wasn't just luck; it was a bold move into a then-emerging digital currency. Erik's story emphasizes the potential of recognizing trends and having the courage to invest early.

- **Connor Bruggemann.** Trading penny stocks might sound risky, but Connor's success highlights the importance of education and strategy. He didn't just throw money at random stocks; he understood the market and refined his skills.

- **Robert Mfune.** As a teen, he scored with trading stocks using a strategy known as "options." Proving you can rock at investing, even at a young age. His success highlights the value of diversifying one's approach to investments and the potential rewards of gaining knowledge in less conventional areas.

- **Brittany Wenger.** By investing her time and intellect, Brittany helped create a groundbreaking app that detects breast cancer. She demonstrated that investments can extend beyond financial means. The success of her app showcases the value of combining passion with purpose.

- **Ben Pasternak.** Ben's journey from developing a viral game to moving into the startup world reflects the entrepreneurial spirit. It's a testament to how innovation and creativity can be valuable assets in the tech industry.

As you can see, anyone, regardless of age, can hit a grand slam. These young business leaders have one thing in common: They weren't afraid to find an opportunity and go with it. What's stopping you from doing the same? You can find money-making chances within your own skills, knowledge, and abilities. It's all a question of finding something you're passionate about and putting in the work.

Trust me. If others can do it, you can, too.

Understanding Risk vs. Reward

Every venture, whether traditional or unconventional, comes with risks. Don't be swayed by the latest trends or viral stocks. Do your research, understand the market dynamics, and resist the temptation to invest money you can't afford to lose. In the investment world, impulsive decisions often lead to pitfalls. When it comes to unpredictable markets like crypto, patience is your best friend. In personal projects, you might face challenges in gaining visibility or attracting customers. When investing in brands or passions, market fluctuations or company changes can impact stock prices. The key is to set realistic expectations, diversify your efforts, and be prepared to adapt. Think about the big picture, develop a long-term game plan, and know that it's totally fine to pace yourself and not rush things.

It's also important to remember, if it seems too good to be true, it likely is. Investing your hard-earned dollars into a scheme promising overnight success is probably not a good idea. In those cases, the risk isn't worth the reward. On the flip side, safer investments such as mutual funds or bonds, offer lower risk but won't make you a millionaire overnight. In the investment world, slow and steady wins the race. "Slow and steady" means your investment is much safer. The main thing to keep in mind is patience.

Now, I don't want you to be afraid of risk. The idea is to feel empowered enough to embrace risk instead of fearing it. But I do want you to keep a level head. Keep your cool and focus your attention. I know that some so-called investments out there sound awesome. I mean, they promise you the moon and the stars. But always remember to slam the brakes and take a minute to think about what you're doing. Oftentimes, chilling out for a second as you think things through is the best way to keep you from making unnecessary financial mistakes.

If you're ever in doubt, ask someone you trust for their opinion. Bouncing your ideas off someone else can be the best way to keep risk on the sidelines. After all, how many superheroes jump head-first into an adventure? They always have a trusty sidekick to alert them of possible dangers. So, let others play Robin to your investment Batman. Trust me. You'll appreciate an honest opinion in times of doubt.

Get Started Today

Investing is a powerful tool for financial growth. Think of it as planting seeds for your future wealth. When you invest wisely, whether in mutual funds, business opportunities, or stocks, you're essentially watering these seeds. The goal is to ensure that your invested money is as productive and hardworking as you are. Check out Page 20 of your bonus workbook for a handy checklist of 12 steps to help you get started.

Another fantastic way to dip your toes into investing without the risk is through "paper trading." Many platforms offer simulated trading experiences where you can practice buying and selling stocks, with fake money. This virtual trading environment lets you experience the market's ups and downs, test out strategies, and gain confidence—all without risking your actual cash. It's an excellent option for beginners to get a feel for the market dynamics and learn the ropes of investing. Think of it as the ultimate investment rehearsal, preparing you for the real deal. Platforms like TD Ameritrade, E*TRADE and TradeStation are just a few that offer this simulated experience for beginners.

Finally, as a gentle reminder, managing risk is crucial while investing. There are tons of ways you can mess things up, so it's always best to chat with folks who've been around the block. We all make mistakes, but the idea here is to dodge the expensive ones, that most of us have already stumbled into. Learn from our slip-ups and don't rush in blindly. Taking the time to do your homework can be the difference between watching your investments grow tall or seeing them shrivel up. And in case you need a refresher, you can find a helpful investing cheat sheet on Page 19 of your workbook.

Next Up

As we leave the world of investing behind, feeling smarter about making our money grow, it's time to tackle something a bit less exciting but super important: taxes and insurance. Up next, we're diving into what Uncle Sam doesn't want you to know. In the next chapter we'll shed light on why we pay taxes, the different kinds that nibble away at our wallets, and why insurance isn't just another bill but a necessity. We'll clarify some misconceptions about taxes and share tips on how to keep more of your money.

Have you ever wondered why a chunk of your paycheck disappears before you even see it or what type of insurance you actually need? We've got you covered. See you in the next Chapter!

Before We Move On... Would You Help Encourage Others?

Our goal is to make learning about money more accessible and easier for everyone. This book is meant to help the curious teenagers and the proactive parents and educators, looking to improve money skills in our youth. But in order to reach them, I need your help. You see, people often choose which books to read based on what others say about it. Yep, reviews matter... A LOT! Reviews are so incredibly helpful to us Authors who are trying to get resources out to those who need it most. So, here's my big ask for you. Would you consider leaving a review for this book? It would mean the world to me.

If you're excited to help someone you've never met, then welcome to the club of amazing people who are making a difference. It's super easy! Just scan this QR code and share your thoughts:

Or Access The Link Here:
https://geni.us/msft-review

P.S. When you share something valuable, you become a hero in someone's story. If you think this book can help another parent or teen, why not spread the joy and recommend it to them?

"The smallest act of kindness is worth more than the grandest intention"
– Oscar Wilde

9

What Uncle Sam Doesn't Want You to Know

Benjamin Franklin once said, "In this world, nothing can be said to be certain except death and taxes." Now, obviously, we can't do much about death. But as far as taxes go, there's plenty we can do. There are smart ways to handle them to ensure we pay our fair share without breaking any rules. But here's the thing: we *only* want to pay our fair share and not a penny more.

That's what this chapter is about. Developing a game plan that will enable you to pay what you owe and still have enough left for the fun stuff. While taxes may seem complicated, we'll help simplify them to enhance your understanding and expand your knowledge.

Taxes – Let's Start with the Basics

Oh, the joy of taxes. I'm sure you've heard folks grumble about them. But do you know why taxes even exist? Do you understand *why* we have to pay them? Or do you know how much your fair share is? Let's jump in!

Why Do We Pay Taxes?

Think of taxes as the financial glue that holds our community together. Ultimately, they're contributions we make to our cities and government. The idea of taxation goes way back, and it's more than just some red-tape invention to make our lives more complicated. They go into a shared pot and help fund things like schools, roads, and other important stuff. Imagine your tax dollars as tiny superheroes who work behind the scenes to keep your community running smoothly.

Take schools, for example. Your taxes help pay for teachers, textbooks, and those colorful bulletin boards in the hallways. Ever noticed the freshly paved roads or the smooth flow of traffic lights? That's your tax money hard at work, making your daily commute a little less bumpy.

Let's not forget that local park where you may go for a jog or enjoy a lazy Sunday hangout. The neatly trimmed grass, playground equipment, the paved walkways—all funded by taxes. Your dollars contribute to creating and maintaining these shared spaces where you can relax and unwind.

Taxes are also like an investment in the future. They fund research, innovation, and community programs that benefit everyone. So, when you hear about a new library opening or a fun community event, you can bet that taxes are playing a starring role somewhere in the background.

In some countries, taxes also play an important role in supporting the healthcare system. They help provide free or affordable medical care that people have come to rely on. This means you can get the healthcare you need without worrying about the cost, thanks to the tax contributions from everyone in the community.

Sure, taxes may just feel like an extra chunk taken out of your paycheck. But ultimately, they do come back to you through improved services, infrastructure, and a generally better quality of life. So, the next time you grumble about taxes, remember, they're the unsung heroes making your community more functional and vibrant.

Types of Taxes

The term "taxes" is a general term used to refer to the money you pay to the government to finance all the cool stuff we talked about earlier. However, not all taxes are alike. Let's chat about the different types of taxes you may need to pay at one point or another.

Income Tax

First up, we've got income tax. This one is a sneak peek into adulthood because it kicks in when you start to earn your own money. A slice of that paycheck you receive from your part-time gig or summer job will go to the government in the form of taxes. Think of it like a tiny responsibility tag that comes along with earning money.

Additionally, if you live in the US, you may come across federal and state income taxes. Federal income tax is imposed by the federal government on your earnings, while state income tax is enforced by the state government. These taxes are calculated based on your income and may vary depending on the state you live in.

Social Security

In some countries you will find social security contributions, deducted from your paycheck. These help cover retirement pensions but also, in some cases, health insurance and medical care.

Healthcare Taxes

In the U.S., you might see a Medicare tax deducted from your paycheck. It funds the federal Medicare program, which provides healthcare for people over 65 and for certain younger people with disabilities. In the UK, you will likely find National Insurance contributions, deducted from your wages. These help fund the National Health Service (NHS) along with other state benefits. Other countries may also have specific "levies" or taxes dedicated to funding health insurance or healthcare services, which might be reflected as a separate line-item on your paycheck.

Understanding and appreciating these healthcare taxes is crucial, as they play a vital role in ensuring that essential healthcare services are accessible to those in need, contributing to the overall health and wellbeing of our communities.

Sales Tax

Now, let's talk about sales tax. Let's say you're eyeing a new video game or the latest cosmetic product. When you march up to the counter to make your purchase, I'm sure you've noticed that the price tag is not the final word. There's this thing called sales tax that gets added on. It's like a little extra fee that goes straight into the government's piggy bank. It can be a buzzkill, but it's a necessary evil to help make our world work and something we, as adults, must accept and plan for.

Property Tax

Now, you might not be a homeowner just yet, but you will be one day, so it's important to understand these taxes. When people own houses or land, they pay property tax. Think of it as a membership fee for having a place to call your own. Property tax helps fund local services like schools and community projects, making your neighborhood an awesome place to live.

All About Tax Brackets

Alright, let's dive into the world of tax brackets – the not-so-secret pathway that determines how much of your hard-earned cash gets to stay with you. Think of it like a financial rollercoaster but with less screaming and more number crunching.

Here's the lowdown: Tax brackets are like income neighborhoods. As you climb the income ladder, you move into different neighborhoods, each with its own tax rate.

First stop: **The "Low Income" Hood**. This is where you start, and it's all sunshine and rainbows (well, relatively speaking). You pay the lowest tax rate on your earnings, usually around 10% to 15%, depending on your country's specific tax laws. It's like the government saying, "Hey, we get it. You're just starting out, so we won't take too much of your pizza money."

Next up: **The "Middle Class" District**. As your paychecks start to increase, you'll enter this next bracket. Here, the tax rate climbs to between 15% to 25%. You're earning more, but still enjoying the fruits of your labor. It's like upgrading from a regular coffee to a fancy latte – a bit pricier, but within reason.

Then, we hit the **"High Income" Territory**. A harsh reality of the tax world; the more you earn, the more taxes you pay. Some would say it's the cost of success. Tax rates in this neighborhood range from 25% to 35%. When you can afford those fancy dinners and luxury items, you're expected to chip in more to the tax pot.

Lastly, the **"High Roller" Penthouse**. Think of it as the peak of the financial mountain where tax rates hit their highest. When you're raking in the big bucks, you're essentially lounging in the penthouse of earnings. Sure, the tax rate is steeper up here, and can be up to

40% of your income, but it's all fair game when you're playing in the big leagues. You know what they say; with great financial power comes great responsibility – or something like that.

Getting a grip on tax brackets is like unlocking a cheat code for your finances. By knowing which "neighborhood" you're in, you can better strategize your finances, ensuring you're prepared for tax time and making the most of your hard-earned money.

Common Mistakes and Misconceptions

The time has now come to debunk some common tax myths and misconceptions. Some of these may seem foreign to you now, but they will be important to keep in mind as you start earning more money.

Myth #1: "Taxes are optional – they'll never catch me."

Wishful thinking. Taxes are like the ultimate game of hide-and-seek, where the government always wins. Trying to dodge taxes? That's a major no-go. It could lead to serious consequences ranging from hefty fines to cozy stays in not-so-cozy places. Trust me, it's better to play it safe and square up with your taxes.

Myth #2: "I don't make enough to pay taxes, so I don't need to file."

Hold up. You might still need to file taxes even if you're not flexing a fancy lifestyle. Remember the brackets we talked about earlier. Each bracket has an income threshold, and even with a minimum wage job, you could still fall into one of them. Not filing when you should can lead to missed opportunities for tax credits or benefits. You don't want to leave money on the table!

Myth #3: "I don't need to report all my income – just the big stuff."

Reality check: Uncle Sam wants to know about all your financial adventures, big or small. From that side hustle cash to the tips you make delivering pizza. Hiding income could land you in hot water. Be honest about your income and remember, the IRS always has its detective hat on.

Now, why does it matter so much to get your taxes right? Well, aside from keeping the taxman off your back, it's about being a responsible member of society.

If the tax world starts looking like a maze of confusion, don't sweat it. That's where the tax pros come in. Seeking professional help is like having Google Maps for taxes – they guide you through the twists and turns, ensuring you don't wind up lost in a sea of forms.

Investing in tax education is another smart move. It's like learning the rules of a game before playing. Understanding the basics helps you make informed decisions and prevents those "uh-oh" moments during tax season.

Insurance – What Is It and Why We Need It

Okay, so what's insurance all about? You've likely heard the term tossed around, but what exactly does it mean? Let's unpack why insurance is such a crucial part of our lives.

What Is Insurance?

Insurance is that financial safety net, that we hope we never have to use, but are deeply thankful for when it becomes necessary. At its core, insurance is like having a trusty umbrella on a rainy day – it's there to shield you from life's unexpected downpours. And what happens when you need it but don't have it? Well, unfortunately, you could be in a world of hurt.

Financial Protection – Your Shield Against the Storm

Think of life as a game of chess, and risks are your opponent's unpredictable moves. Now, you can't control every move, but you can strategize to minimize the impact. That's where risk management comes in.

Insurance is like your master chess move. It helps prepare you for life's unexpected events. When you're hit with unexpected medical bills or a fender bender that crinkles more than just your bumper, insurance steps in to shine. It won't stop the rain but will keep you from getting soaked.

Consider this situation:

You've got health insurance guarding your well-being, home insurance protecting your casa, and auto insurance covering you on the road. It's like having a team of superheroes standing by, ready to swoop in and save the day when life takes an unexpected turn. As I mentioned earlier, you get insurance, hoping you'll never need it. But when you do, knowing you're covered is an amazing feeling.

Types of Insurance

Now, keep in mind that not all insurance coverages are the same. Here is a look at the different types of coverages you can typically find:

- **Health Insurance.** It's like your personal health bodyguard. When you face a medical hiccup, health insurance steps in to help foot the bill, ensuring you can focus on recovery rather than worrying about the cost.

- **Auto Insurance.** Your road trip companion, defending you against unexpected bumps in the road. From minor scrapes to major collisions, auto insurance has your back, making sure you're not left in a financial ditch.

- **Home Insurance.** Think of it as your home's knight in shining armor. Whether it's a burglary, fire, or a leaky roof, home insurance cushions the financial blow, so you're not left picking up the pieces alone.

- **Renters Insurance.** As a teenager, it's essential to familiarize yourself with renters insurance, especially as you begin to venture into independent living. When you move out and find your own apartment, renters insurance can offer valuable protection for both you and your belongings.

Depending on your life and needs, you might have to get additional coverage for your business, special gear (like musical instruments or expensive equipment), or coverage for your furry companions. Never forget that insurance buys peace of mind. Sure, it can be tough to shell out the monthly payments. But take my word for it. You don't want to go without insurance, and you must plan for it as you enter adulthood.

Insurance Lingo

Let's break down some of the common lingo you'll find in the insurance world:

Premiums – The Regular Dues

Consider premiums as regular installments, similar to a subscription fee, for a service that provides financial protection and peace of mind. You pay a set amount, usually monthly or annually, to keep your coverage active.

Scenario: Let's say you have car insurance. Your premium is the fee for the ongoing protection of your vehicle. Paying it ensures your car insurance is always ready to act when needed.

Deductibles – Your Initial Investment

Deductibles are like the amount you agree to cover in the case of a claim before the insurance kicks in. It's your financial skin in the game. Think of it as the down payment on a shopping spree, but in this case, it's for unexpected events.

Scenario: You get into a fender bender, and there's $500 in damages. If your auto insurance has a $250 deductible, you're responsible for that first $250, and your insurance covers the rest. It's your way of saying, "I'm in for this much. Now let's fix this."

Claims – Calling in the Calvary

Claims are when you call up your insurance agents for help. You've experienced a situation that requires your insurance's help. Now it's time to cash in on that financial protection you've been diligently paying for. It's like using the insurance safety net when life throws you a curveball.

Scenario: Let's say you misjudged the distance and backed into that parking meter, resulting in minor damage to your vehicle. You file a claim with your car insurance, and they swing into action to cover the costs of repairs. It's your insurance stepping up to mend the situation.

These terms will come in handy whenever you review an insurance policy. So, keep them in mind as you learn more about insurance.

Maximizing What You Keep in Your Pocket

Ready for a crash course in deductions, credits, and savvy strategies to make the most of your financial situation?

The Magic of Deductions and Credits

Imagine deductions and credits as your secret weapons against the taxman – they're your way of keeping more money in your pocket.

Everyone gets a standard deduction, which is like a tax-free gift. However, if your parents claim you as a dependent, the rules might change slightly. This is why you may want to look at the silver lining and consider the perks of an "independent" status. Essentially, you may be eligible for larger deductions and credits, putting more money back into your wallet, if you opt to break free from your parents' "dependent" status.

Strategies to Trim Taxable Income

Now, let's discuss some smart strategies to reduce your taxable income and maximize your returns.

- Traditional and Roth IRA Accounts. Investing in your future while potentially snagging a "savers credit"? Yes, please! As we spoke about in Chapter 5, Traditional 401(k) or IRA retirement accounts can reduce your taxable income today, while Roth IRAs can set you up for tax-free withdrawals in the future. Review your bonus workbook, for a refresher on retirement plan options.

- Education Savings Plans (such as 529 or ESA Accounts): These are a treasure chest for educational expenses. Contribute to them, and not only are you preparing for the future, but you might also score some tax benefits today.

- Health Savings Accounts (HSAs): A health-savvy move! Contributions to an HSA can lower your taxable income while creating a financial cushion for future medical expenses.

- Educational Expenses: If college is on the horizon, educational expenses can be a golden ticket for tax breaks. Look into the "American Opportunity Credit" (also known as "AOTC") and the "Lifetime Learning Credit" (also known as "LLC"). They're specifically built for students to help ease the financial burden of higher education. You can find great

resources on the irs.gov website to read more about these programs:
https://www.eitc.irs.gov/other-refundable-credits-toolkit/what-you-need-to-know-about-aotc-and-llc/what-you-need-to-know

Advanced Strategies for Tax Efficiency

If you're getting into investing or launching your own business, there are some additional tax tips you should consider. These tips help you hold onto more of your hard-earned money. By staying informed and making wise decisions, you can reduce what you owe in taxes and keep more cash in your pocket.

For those dabbling in investing, try to hold onto your investments for over a year. This way, you'll pay less tax through something called long-term capital gains. The government taxes profits from investments held for over a year at a lower rate than profits from investments sold within a year of buying them. It's like making your money work smarter, not harder.

And for the overachiever hustlers with a side gig, keep a close eye on those business expenses. If you're self-employed, itemizing deductions can be a game-changer. Anything you need to spend money on to get your business started or keep it running, you can write off as a business expense. Consider leveraging your passion project as a smart tax-saving strategy.

Remember, Uncle Sam has a ton of tax breaks out there for you to take advantage of; you just have to know where to look and how to use them. For a quick reference of the most common tax tips, check out Page 21 of your bonus workbook, titled "Tax Tips."

Real-Life Examples of Tax-Saving Strategies

Let's break down the tax tale of two scenarios – one without any tax-saving wizardry and the other where our savvy teen taps into some smart financial moves. Get ready for a journey into the world of numbers, deductions, and potential savings!

Scenario 1: No Tax Savings Techniques

Meet Sean. He pulled in a whopping $36,000 last year at his part-time job. So, he has a gross income of $36,000. After taking the standard deduction for a single filer in 2023 (which was $13,850), he ended up with a taxable income of $22,150. Now, considering the tax bracket that Sean fell into, the taxes he owed totaled $2,560. That's a hefty sum that he has to say goodbye to.

Scenario 2: Using Tax Savings Techniques

Now let's add some magic to the mix. Sean has decided to play the tax game a bit more strategically.

- He contributes $3,000 to a Traditional IRA retirement account. Along with his standard single filer deduction, this brings his taxable income down to $19,150.

- He also spent $1,000 in books and tuition, making him eligible for the American Opportunity Credit. This credit can be a dollar-for-dollar reduction of taxes owed, up to a $2,500 credit. So in this case Sean has a full $1,000 credit, because of his qualified educational expenses.

With his taxable income now at $19,150, the new total taxes owed is $2,197. But wait, remember the American Opportunity Credit? That also swoops in and reduces that amount even further by $1,000. Now, Sean is left with a total tax owed of only $1,197.

Comparison:

- Without tax-saving techniques: Taxes Owed = $2,560

- With tax-saving techniques: Taxes Owed = $1,197

For a Total Savings Of: $1,363

Yes, you read that right. By strategically using tax-saving techniques, Sean saved over $1,000 on his taxes. That's money back in his pocket for future adventures, investments, or just a little extra padding for peace of mind.

This example proves the power of understanding and utilizing available tax credits, deductions, and other opportunities. It's not about outsmarting the system but making it work for you. So, when tax season rolls around, remember a little financial strategy can go a long way in keeping more of your hard-earned dollars where they belong – with you.

Next Up

OK, now that you have this knowledge tucked under your belt, think of it like a magic spell card you can play when needed. Knowing about taxes will help you keep more of your cash in your pocket. And having the lowdown on insurance will help keep you safe when you need it most.

So, what's next?

In our next and final chapter, you'll learn about the secrets to getting a "YES." It's all about mastering the art of communication. We'll explore strategies to manage challenging conversations effectively and techniques to sway your parents (or anyone for that matter) to not only listen to your ideas but also be more likely to agree with them. Say goodbye to those instant 'NO's and learn how to turn them into 'YES's! Are you ready?

10

The Secret Sauce – The Key to Getting a "YES"

B y this point, we've established a solid foundation for what will eventually grow into your financial success. Can you picture yourself confidently managing your finances? Are you excited to implement what you've learned and see what kind of smart money moves you can make?

I hope so! But there's one final topic we need to talk about. As the title of this chapter implies, this is the secret sauce. The power of persuasion.

Mastering the power of persuasion helps unlock the all-powerful "YES." Like Steve Jobs once said, "People don't know what they want until you show it to them."

In this chapter, you'll learn how to understand and show people what they want. Perfecting this skill can significantly increase your chances of achieving your goals. Let's find out how to build a memorable message that wins every time.

The Psychology Behind a Yes

People's minds are naturally incredibly active, filled with countless thoughts and ideas. Ever notice how those non-stop thoughts zip through your brain, like scrolling through TikTok at lightning speed? Sometimes, it's like trying to follow a group chat that's blowing up your phone – hard to keep up, right?

Trying to get people to see things your way can make their brains go into turbo mode, and their natural reaction might be to become defensive. It's a survival instinct. Something we've had ingrained in our minds since the beginning of time.

That defense mechanism creates a tough barrier to break. And that barrier can lead to a number of challenging reactions. For example, salespeople often receive an automatic "no" when they try to pitch something. People naturally distrust folks in sales, especially when they don't look or feel too trustworthy.

So, how can you get people to listen to you? It all boils down to trust. When people trust you, they tend to agree with you. However, if they don't, you may struggle to get them on your side.

Think about lawyers. What do they do in court? Defense lawyers try their best to schmooze the jury so they favor their side of the case. And what do prosecutors do? They look serious and sure of themselves. They try to convince the jury that they have all the evidence to convict the defendant. Both sides are trying to win over the jury, in their own strategic ways. Ultimately, the secret sauce to earning that "yes" is trust.

But there's more to trust than just looking or sounding sure of yourself. Let's explore more.

Principles of Influence and Persuasion

Robert Cialdini is a well-known author and researcher who knows a lot about influence and persuasion[1]. His work has led to the principles that some of the most successful and influential people follow down to the letter. Let's break down those principles and get you up-to-speed on them.

Reciprocity

Aside from being hard to say, reciprocity is like a social tango where one kind action leads to another in return. It's an unwritten rule that nudges us to return a favor when someone has helped us out. Take a scenario where a classmate lends you their notes for a missed class. You may want to reciprocate the gesture and help them with something, perhaps by offering to tutor them on a challenging subject. It's a social exchange that keeps the cycle of kindness flowing.

Commitment and Consistency

Commitment and consistency form the backbone of reliability. Once someone decides to take action on something, there's an internal and external pressure to stay true to that commitment. As a teenager, it may be publicly committing to a goal like running for student council or joining a club. It often results in following through as you've announced your intentions to classmates, friends, or family. Or maybe a friend persuades you to promise that you'll go to a party. Just by saying "maybe" increases the likelihood of you following through and actually going to the party.

Social Proof

Social Proof is essentially the concept of "following the crowd." Or the bandwagon effect, as some like to call it. When people are unsure of what to do, they often look to others to influence their actions. For instance, if a new movie or app is all the rage, it creates a ripple effect, enticing more people to check it out. Or suppose your classmates are all talking about or participating in a school event. The hype will naturally encourage more students to want to join in, right?

Authority

Authority is the magnetism of influence. Teens often gravitate toward figures of authority or those who are deemed experts. For example, younger students are likelier to follow suit if a respected senior or teacher supports a school event. Or, in today's digital age, social media influencers may have a similar "authoritative" role in shaping your opinions.

Liking

Liking is the magic ingredient in persuasion. Simply put, people are more easily swayed by those they like. Imagine if that crush of yours recommends trying out a new restaurant; how eager do you think you'd be to check it out? You'd probably be putting it into your GPS, as soon as school gets out! Recommendations and invitations from friends carry significant weight, creating a persuasive atmosphere grounded in personal connections.

Scarcity

Scarcity makes things seem more valuable because they're harder to get. Opportunities become more tempting when they seem rare or exclusive. For example, you might rush to buy concert tickets if you hear they're "almost sold out." Or make an unplanned trip to Ulta for that "limited time only" product.

Emotions

Emotions are the captains of decision-making. They direct the entire process, subtly guiding our choices and actions. Understanding the science of persuasion involves recognizing the powerful role emotions play. Whether it's the joy of reciprocating, the pride in consistency, the thrill of being part of a trend, the respect for authority, the warmth of liking, or the fear of missing out, emotions act as the driving force behind the choices we make and the influence we give in to.

Crafting the Perfect Pitch

Now, it's your moment to persuade others to embrace your ideas. You may want to sell something or get others on board with your plans. But how will you do it?

Key Components of a Perfect and Persuasive Pitch

Let's break down the anatomy of an irresistible and convincing pitch. Picture it as a recipe for success – a blend of ingredients ensuring your pitch is not only heard but genuinely impactful.

- **A Captivating Introduction.** Think of your introduction as the opening scene of an epic movie. You've got to grab attention fast. Start with a compelling story, a surprising fact, or a thought-provoking question. Make your audience lean into your words.

- **Clear and Concise Problem Statement.** Clearly explain the problem you're addressing. Imagine you're handing someone a jigsaw puzzle – show them the pieces, make them understand the challenge, and why it's worth solving. But keep it short and sweet; nobody wants to drown in a word tsunami.

- **Your Solution – The Hero.** Now, present your solution as the hero coming to the rescue. Explain how your idea, product, or service is the missing piece that solves the puzzle. Use props if possible – charts, graphs, or even a demo. Make it easy for your audience to visualize success.

- **Benefits, Not Features.** Don't just list features; highlight the real-world benefits. Translate the capabilities or technicalities into clear advantages. For example, if you're applying for a job, it may not just be about your grades or the clubs you're in; it's about how your unique strengths can bring fresh ideas or make a team vibe better.

- **Know Your Audience.** Understand who you're pitching to and tailor it to focus on what *they* care about. If you're trying to impress a potential employer, highlight how you'll be a game-changer at their company. Or if you're asking your parents for something, explain how it benefits the whole family, not just you. Or maybe you're trying to sell something; focus on how your product simplifies your customer's life.

- **Social Proof – Your Wingman.** Bring in testimonials, success stories, references, or any evidence that supports your idea. If someone else has invested, used, or benefited from your pitch, shout it from the rooftops (or at least from PowerPoint slides). If you're pitching yourself to employers, make sure you have a few references lined up who can speak to how awesome you are.

- **Handle Objections Before They Arise.** Anticipate your audience's questions, concerns, and objections. By doing so, you can be ready to address them head-on. It shows that you've done your homework and boosts your credibility. Turn potential roadblocks into stepping stones.

- **Compelling Call to Action.** What do you want your audience to do after your pitch? Whether it's saying "yes," buying your product or hiring you, make your call to action crystal clear. If appropriate, create a sense of urgency and leave them with a clear next step.

- **Passion and Authenticity.** Your enthusiasm is contagious. Let the love for your idea shine through. Authenticity is your secret sauce – people can sense it and they eat it up. Tell them why you believe in what you're pitching; let them feel the heartbeat behind your words.

- **Be Unforgettable – Leave a Lasting Impression.** Aim to be memorable. You don't want your pitch to fade into the background noise. Think of a memorable tagline, a striking image, or a compelling closing statement that lingers in the minds of your listeners.

Remember that the perfect pitch is about creating a connection with your audience. Don't just dump information on them or try to razzle dazzle them. Instead, look for a genuine understanding. Your sincerity is what closes the deal every time.

The Power of Body Language

There's an unsung hero in communication: body language. Your body language can make a big difference between getting people to go along with you or a crash-and-burn scenario. Let's look at how body language can be an ace up your sleeve.

Silent Melody

Ever heard the phrase "actions speak louder than words"? Well, it's not just a catchy line. Your body language is like a quiet soundtrack accompanying your speech; it can either sync up perfectly or clash with what you're trying to say. It plays a vital role in the communication dance.

The Non-Verbal Band

Picture this: you're passionately sharing your brilliant idea, but your arms are crossed, creating an unintentional stand-offish vibe. Or, while explaining the perks of your product, your nervous foot-tapping steals the spotlight and becomes a distraction. Non-verbal cues can either boost your message or completely overshadow it.

Tips and Tricks to Strike the Right Chord

First up, eye contact. It may be challenging for some, but it's so important to remember. Try to maintain good eye contact with your audience. But don't turn it into a stare-down contest; that's just creepy. Next, keep your posture open and confident; slouching sends the wrong message. Finally, don't forget to smile – it's a universal language of friendliness.

Another pro-tip is mirroring. Practice subtly mimicking the body language of your audience. It helps build rapport. And what about gestures? Use them, but don't go Broadway. A well-timed gesture can emphasize a point, but flailing arms distract from your message.

Dos and Don'ts of Body Language

Dos:

- Stand or sit up straight. It screams confidence.

- Use purposeful gestures. They can emphasize your words.

- Align your facial expressions to the tone of your message.

- Maintain eye contact. It shows respect for your audience.

Don'ts

- Cross your arms. It's a barricade to connecting.

- Fidget excessively. It's distracting for the audience.

- Avoid eye contact. It makes you seem disengaged or untrustworthy.

Keep in mind that less is more. You might be tempted to put on a song and dance to get people on board with your ideas. But staying cool and keeping it real is the ultimate winning ticket. There's no need to go overboard when you've masterfully created a killer sales pitch and have the confidence to stand by it.

The Art of Storytelling

Who doesn't love a good story? Often, the key to persuasion lies in crafting an unforgettable story. Think of it as the secret formula that ensures your message hits home and stays with your audience. Storytelling is a critical component in any successful pitch. Here's a tip for making your stories impactful:

Instead of bombarding someone with a bunch of dry facts and figures, try weaving them into a creative narrative. Something that takes your audience on an adventure. That's the essence of storytelling – turning ordinary information into something extraordinary and memorable.

While facts can be like puzzle pieces, storytelling is the glue that holds them together. Stories evoke emotions, create connections, and make information relatable. It's not just about delivering the data; it's about activating the feels. When your audience feels a connection, they're not just hearing your message; they're experiencing it.

So, how do you build a narrative that resonates? Start with a compelling beginning—something that grabs attention. It could be a story, a relatable scenario, or even a question. Once you have their attention, take them on a journey. Introduce characters, conflicts, and resolutions. Make it a rollercoaster of emotions.

Keep in mind that simplicity is the golden rule. Break down complicated ideas into bite-sized pieces, like chapters in a book. It helps your audience follow along and stay engaged. Use vivid language, like descriptive and expressive words, to paint a mental picture. When people can visualize your message, it becomes etched in their memory.

Here's another pro tip: be authentic. Share personal experiences or real-life examples. Being genuine creates trust and connects with people on a deeper level. It adds a human touch to your message, transforming it from mere information into a meaningful experience.

Finally, end with impact. Leave your audience with something to think about, whether it's a powerful conclusion or a call to action. And make them feel like they've gained something of value from their time with you.

When you nail these essential aspects, you can spin a tale that transforms your pitch into a masterpiece. Be sure to take the time to polish your approach until it flows effortlessly and you feel confident delivering it to any audience.

Overcoming Objections and Breaking Down Roadblocks

It's no secret that teenagers often find themselves in situations where they feel they must defend their choices or opinions. It could be a disagreement with parents, a debate with friends, or even a challenge from a teacher. So, what do you do when faced with objections?

One key strategy is *understanding* the objection. Instead of immediately going on the defense, take a moment to really try to grasp where the other person is coming from. Active listening is your best friend here. The idea is that once you understand their perspective, you can respond more effectively.

Try to practice role-playing scenarios. When you practice handling objections, you strengthen your ability to respond effectively. Team up with a friend or a sibling, or even practice on your own by playing out both sides of the conversation. This way, you can test different responses in a safe environment. It's like preparing for a conversational marathon—you want to be ready for anything.

Staying calm and composed is the key to effective communication when faced with skepticism or doubt. Easier said than done, right? Take a deep breath, gather your thoughts, and respond thoughtfully. Remember, it's not about winning an argument; it's about active listening and expressing your perspective in a manner that promotes mutual understanding.

Another strategy is acknowledging the doubt without getting defensive. Taking a moment to say something as simple as, "I see where you're coming from, and I appreciate your concern," shows maturity and opens the door for a more constructive conversation.

Here's a fun fact; throwing a little humor into a conversation tends to lighten the mood. A well-timed joke or a light-hearted comment can diffuse tension and create a more positive atmosphere. Just be careful not to use it as a way to deflect serious issues.

Real-World Example of Crafting the Perfect Pitch

Meet Jamie, an ambitious 18-year-old with a plan. She's got her eyes set on a gap year filled with adventures and travel before diving into the college world. But, there's a hurdle—convincing her parents. Let's peek into Jamie's strategy for tackling her pitch.

Trust and Credibility

First up, Jamie understands the power of trust and credibility. Armed with research, she showers her parents with case studies of successful individuals who've triumphed academically and professionally after a gap year. It's like saying, "Look, it worked for them; it can work for me too!"

FOMO

Jamie also taps into the psychology behind Fear of Missing Out. She vividly describes unique opportunities available only during this potential gap year timeframe. Volunteer programs and travel experiences crafted for young adults are not to be missed. It's the 'carpe diem' card, and she's playing it well.

A Sprinkle of Magic

Now, let's sprinkle a bit of Cialdini's magic. Jamie, being a proficient persuader, pulls out the reciprocity card. She sweetens the deal by offering to chip in and pay for a portion of her adventure from her own savings. If you help me, I'll help you! A win-win that eases the financial burden on her parents.

Commitment

Commitment is her next move. Jamie promises to defer her college acceptance, delaying her start date by only a year. Locking in her attendance after the gap year. It's a strategic play to reassure her parents that this isn't a detour but a planned pitstop on the road to success.

Social Proof

Social proof? Jamie's got it covered. She drops names and stories of friends who've had enriching gap year experiences. Something like this; "Remember Mike? He traveled to the Philippines during his gap year and helped with a home-building project. He got to help a community in need while meeting some amazing people. He even picked up some new skills. He said it was a once-in-a-lifetime experience." I mean, who could say no to that?!

Liking

Jamie adds a personal touch by tapping into her history of responsible decision-making, reassuring her parents that she has consistently shown good judgment. She also gently reminds them that their exceptional parenting played a significant role in fueling her ambition and eagerness for experiences such as this. It's not just about facts; it's a reflection of the bond she shares with her parents.

An Emotional Touch

Now for the emotional finale. Jamie bares her soul, expressing her burning passion for understanding different cultures and the heartfelt desire to give back through volunteering. She connects the dots between this experience and how it can shape her future perspective and career. It's a symphony of emotions that resonates strongly with her parents.

The Road Map

Jamie keeps her pitch organized and concise. Guiding her parents through a well-structured plan. She starts with her primary goal and its advantages, followed by details of how it will unfold and the associated costs. Jamie also connects her plan to her future aspirations. To add depth to her proposal, she paints vivid imagery of the breathtaking places she'll explore, the delectable dishes she'll get to try, and the diverse cultures and people she'll get to meet. Creating a captivating visual for her parents.

Her body language remains on point, throughout her pitch. Eyes locked, sitting tall, open hand gestures—she's a picture of confidence. No crossed arms or darting eyes here.

Handling Objections

But Jamie isn't blind to potential roadblocks. Throughout her pitch, she tackles a few expected objections, like "It's a waste of time," "It's not safe," and "You'll be behind your peers." For the first objection, she combats "it's a waste of time" by emphasizing the opportunity for personal growth. For safety? Detailed itinerary and safety measures that are in place. Academic concerns? A gap year can be a guiding tool for selecting her college major, potentially saving time and money in the long run.

Role Playing Perfection

Jamie diligently rehearsed this conversation with a friend. She tried to predict and prepare for any potential objections that might arise. They engaged in multiple practice conversations, honing her ability to respond effectively. So when doubt reared its head, Jamie remained calm and collected. Allowing her to actively listen, address each concern methodically, and ensure the conversation stayed on the right track.

Now It's Your Turn

Alright, let's turn the spotlight on you! Think of something you're passionate about, something you could pitch with enthusiasm. It could be an idea, a project, or even yourself to a potential employer. Below, you'll find some example ideas to get you started. Your bonus workbook also includes a "Principles of Persuasion" cheat sheet. Check out Page 22 for a refresher on the principles discussed in this chapter. After you've had a chance to review everything, I want you to write down your thoughts and craft your pitch. Use the structured worksheets on Pages 23 and 24 of your workbook to put it all together!

Example 1: Pitching an Idea

"Hey! I've been thinking a lot about how we all struggle with keeping up with school assignments, extracurriculars, and personal projects. It feels like we're constantly trying to juggle a million things at once, right? Well, I've come up with a solution that could help us all out (Commitment and Consistency).
I'm developing an app specifically designed for students like us. It's not just any planner app; it's tailored for integrates seamlessly with our unique schedules. What makes it truly unique is its personalized approach to time management, which no other app out there is offering right now (Scarcity).
I plan to launch a beta version soon, but I want to keep the initial

user group small to ensure we can fine-tune everything based on real feedback. This means only a select few will get early access, and I'd love for you to be one of them (Scarcity & Social Proof). I've seen how we all use our phones for pretty much everything, and there's nothing quite like this out there tailored to our needs (more Social Proof).

This app could revolutionize the way we organize our lives. But here's the thing—I need your help to make it even better. Your knack for design and user experience is exactly what I need to take this from a good idea to a great one (Authority). Plus, I've always respected your creativity and insight (Liking). I feel like you might have some brilliant ideas that could seriously elevate this project.

By joining forces, we can create something that is not only useful but also engaging for our peers. Imagine the sense of achievement we'll feel, knowing we're making a real difference in the lives of students just like us, helping them to stay organized and reduce stress (Reciprocity).

I'm super excited about the potential and would love to hear your thoughts. Let's catch up soon and see how we can turn this idea into reality. Thanks for considering this; I really believe together we can create something amazing."

Example 2: Pitching Yourself

"Hello there! I recently learned about your need for a part-time employee and felt compelled to reach out. I've been a loyal customer of yours for years (Reciprocity), and I've always admired how your business serves the community and sets high customer service standards. It's made me want to join your team and contribute to that success.

I've committed myself to excellence in everything I do, both in school projects and volunteer work (Commitment and Consistency). I've seen firsthand how friends and classmates have thrived in part-time jobs, learning valuable skills and building confidence (Social Proof), and I'm eager to follow in their footsteps. I understand the importance of having a knowledgeable and friendly staff, and I've taken the initiative to familiarize myself with your products and services (Authority). My teachers and coaches always commend my positive attitude and my ability to get along well with others (Liking), qualities I know are essential in creating a positive environment for your customers.

I also heard that you're looking to fill this position soon and I feel that someone with my enthusiasm and dedication could really make a difference during the upcoming busy season (Scarcity). I'm ready to start learning and contributing right away, bringing my energy and fresh ideas to your team.

Thank you for considering my application. I look forward to discussing how I can help your team and make a positive impact."

Now, armed with these examples and your own notes and thoughts, take one of your pitches and practice it on someone you trust—a friend, family member, or even a colleague. See how they react, gather feedback, and refine your pitch. Remember, the more you practice, the more confident and persuasive you'll become!

---

1. Cialdini, R. B., & Goldstein, N. J. (2004). Social influence: Compliance and conformity. Annu. Rev. Psychol., 55, 591-621.

THE PERFECT PITCH

Directions: Use the following template to craft your pitch. Remember, try to make a story with emotions, heart and meaning behind your words!

PITCHING YOUR IDEA

What's Your Idea? Write it down and commit to it

What kind of social proof can you show or discuss?

How can you appeal to your audience in a way that makes them want to help you (reciprocate)?

How can you make it more desirable using the scarcity principle (i.e. "Limited Time Offer")?

How can you appeal to your audience to get them to like you?

How can you be (or find) an authoritative figure?

THE PERFECT PITCH

Directions: Use the following template to craft your pitch. Remember, try to make it a story with emotions, heart and meaning behind your words!

PITCHING YOURSELF

Who are you pitching yourself to? Write down it down and commit to it

What kind of social proof (references) can you show or discuss?

How can you appeal to your audience in a way that makes them want to help you (reciprocate)?

How can you make your pitch feel more urgent? What's your call to action?

How can you appeal to your audience to get them to like you?

How can you be (or appeal to) an authoritative figure?

Conclusion

farewell

As we approach the conclusion of this book, I want to express my sincere gratitude for dedicating your time and efforts to these pages.

Throughout these ten chapters, you've been on quite the financial ride. You've picked up vital skills that will hopefully shape how you handle money from now on.

From the basics to making money. Setting goals to learning how to budget. Understanding the importance of savings and spending wisely. Learning new ways to invest and picking up some important nuggets on taxes and credit scores. We've covered *a lot*. And you've handled it like a champ!

We've introduced some essential foundational concepts throughout this book. These concepts are stepping stones to more deeply understanding and mastering your money skills. Take a moment to reflect on which topics sparked your interest the most. Was it investing, budgeting, or the power of persuasion? Whatever caught your eye, I encourage you to dive deeper into those areas. Look for more resources, whether it's books, online courses, or workshops, to further expand your knowledge.

Remember that your financial journey is just starting. With these new skills, you're ready to take on whatever comes your way. Keep that curiosity alive, never stop learning, and watch your financial horizons expand. There's always more to explore!

Be sure to stay tuned for upcoming books and additional resources, all crafted to empower you as you venture further into the world of adulthood. We are committed to supporting you as you continue to grow and prosper.

As we wrap up, remember that you've gained the skills and knowledge to make smarter money choices, secure your financial future, and get closer to your dreams. As you navigate the world armed with this newfound financial wisdom, don't hesitate to grab hold of every opportunity that comes your way.

Again, I want to express my gratitude for choosing "Money Skills for Teens." Here's to your financial well-being, a future brimming with prosperity, and the thrilling adventures waiting for you in your journey ahead!

Want to Help Other Teens?

Our goal is to make learning about money more accessible and easier for everyone. This book is meant to help curious and ambitious teens, just like you, who may not know where to start. But in order to reach them, I need your help. You see, people often choose which books to read based on what others say about it. Yep, reviews matter... A LOT! Reviews are so incredibly helpful to us Authors who are trying to get resources out to those who need it most. So, here's my big ask for you. Would you consider leaving a review for this book? It would mean the world to me.

If you're excited to help someone you've never met, then welcome to the club of awesome people who are making a difference. It's super easy! Just scan this QR code and share your thoughts:

Or Access The Link Here:
https://geni.us/msft-review

P.S. When you share something valuable, you become a hero in someone's story. If you think this book can help another teenager like you, why not spread the joy and recommend it to them?

"The smallest act of kindness is worth more than the grandest intention"
– Oscar Wilde

Thank you ♥

ANSWER KEY

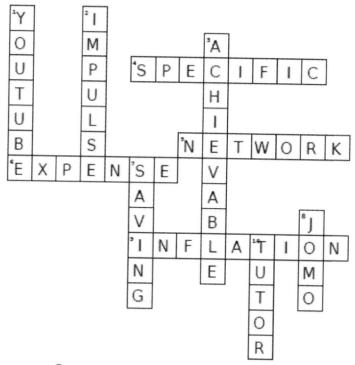

Crossword answers:

1. YOUTUBE (down)
2. IMPULSE (down)
3. ACHIEVABLE (down)
4. SPECIFIC (across)
5. NETWORK (across)
6. EXPENSE (across)
7. SAVING (down)
8. JOMO (down)
9. INFLATION (across)
10. TUTOR (down)

Word search answers: EXPENSE, CREDITCARD, BILLS, BANK, PAYCHECK, SCAM